ROMPER LA BARRERA DEL IDIOMA INGLÉS NIVEL 1
WWW.ELPRINCIPECENTRE.COM
info@elprincipecentre.com

INTRODUCIÓN

Esto es un libro que te ayudará hablar y entender inglés. Ha sido formulado para ayudarte comunicar bien día por día. Te animará en tomar los bloques de construcción del idioma inglés y hacer tus propias frases, preguntas y conversaciones. No es inglés para vacaciones ni de libro de frases. Tampoco te liará con la ciencia de gramatica, más bien te presentará la gramática inglés y español en la forma lo más fácil posible.

Yo he desarrollado este metódo de aprender idiomas después de más de 20 años enseñando ambos inglés y español en España. Sigo creyendo que la mejor forma de aprender algún idioma es asistir clases, pero este libro te sirvirá muy bien para aprender en casa si no tengas oportunidad de tener clases.

Aprender un idioma nuevo no es pequeña cosa. Tarda tiempo y necesita paciencia. La clave es disfrutarlo y no tomarlo tanto en serio. Relájate, disfrútalo, se amable contigo mismo y acepta que lo de equivocarse es una parte del proceso de apender. No tengas mierdo de intentar hablar inglés, aunque digas cosas equivocadas, la clave es comunicar. Si te entiendan, da igual si no digas cada palabra perfectamente.

Fija en lo que has aprendido, no en todavía no sabes, y siempre acuérdate que la perfeción no es possible desde el principio.

Sobre todo, espero que lo disfrutes y encuentres el puro placer en aprender un idioma tan bonito y útil como el inglés, hablado por todo el mundo. En el camino aprenderás mucho de tu propio lenguaje también! Después de este libro, tendrás bastante inglés para tener una conversación básica en inglés, y estarás listo a hacer el Nivel 2.

Good luck!! ☺

Vicki

ROMPER LA BARRERA DEL IDIOMA INGLÉS NIVEL 1
WWW.ELPRINCIPECENTRE.COM
info@elprincipecentre.com

ÍNDICE/ INDEX

	Page Number
1. ABECEDARIO Y PRONUNCIACIÓN	3
2. LOS ARTÍCULOS	9
3. NÚMEROS	11
4. PRACTICA LOS NÚMEROS/ PRACTICE NUMBERS	12
5. ROPA Y NÚMEROS/ CLOTHES AND NUMBERS	13
6. ¿QUÉ HORA ES? / WHAT TIME IS IT?	15
7. EL VERBO "TO BE"- ser/estar/ the verb "to be".	18
8. EL VERBO "TO BE" EN CONTEXTO 1/ THE VERB "TO BE" IN CONTEXT	21
9. EL VERBO "TO BE" EN CONTEXTO 2/ THE VERB "TO BE" IN CONTEXT	23
10. CONVERSACIÓN CON EL VERBO "TO BE"/ CONVERSATION PRACTICE "TO BE"	25
11. DESCRIBIENDO LA GENTE/ DESCRIBING PEOPLE	26
12. HAY/ THERE IS, THERE ARE, IS THERE? ARE THERE?	28
13. HAY/SER/ESTAR/ PRACTICANDO THERE IS/ THERE ARE/ TO BE	29
14. LA CASA DE JOHN/ JOHN´S HOUSE	31
15. VERBOS REGULARES "AR"/ REGULAR VERBS- "AR"	33
16. VERBOS REGULARES "AR" EN CONTEXTO/ IN CONTEXT	52
17. VERBOS REGULARES "ER"/ REGULAR VERBS - "ER"	55
18. VERBOS REGULARES "ER" EN CONTEXTO/ IN CONTEXT	67
19. VERBOS REGULARES "IR"/ REGULAR VERBS- "IR"	70
20. TRADUCCIÓN DE INLGÉS AL ESPAÑOL/ TRANSLATION	82
21. ADVERBIOS DE FRECUENCIA/ ADVERBS OF FREQUENCY	83
22. PRACTICA DE VERBOS REGULARES/PRACTICE OF REGULAR VERBS	84
23. DIPTONGOS/ DIPTHONGS	86
24. DIPTONGOS EN CONTEXTO/ DIPTHONGS IN CONTEXT	110
25. TENER/ TO HAVE	113
26. VERBOS "GO-GO"/ "GO-GO" VERBS	119
27. GUSTAR/ TO LIKE	129
28. GUSTAR/ ENCANTAR/ TO LIKE/ LOVE	132
29. IR/ TO GO	133
30. TIA KATHY/ AUNT KATHY	135
31. POSDATA/ POSTSCRIPT	138
32. CLAVE "TOP TIPS"/ KEY TO "TOP TIPS"	139
33. RESPUESTAS/ ANSWERS	140

1. ABECEDARIO Y PRONUNCIACIÓN

El Abecedario

Se pronuncia el abecedario inglés en una manera muy distincta, y faltan dos letras- no hay "ll" ni "ñ". Tampoco ayuda mucho con la pronunciación de inglés en general. Sin embargo, es importante para deletrear y es esencial saberlo.

PRACTICA A: Escucha los sonidos y practica la pronunciación, notando la diferencia entre español e inglés, especialmente los vocales. (YOUTUBE)

A ehe	N en
B bi	O oh
C si	P pi
D di	Q kiu
E y	R ar
F ehf	S es
G ji	T ti
H jech	U iu
I ay	V vi
J jey	W dublelyu
K key	X ex
L el	Y guay
M em	Z sed

PRACTICA B: Busca que significan estas palabras y después practica pronunciarlas y deletrearlas. (YOUTUBE)

A- "ehe"

   APPLE-

_____

B- "bi"

   BALL-

_____

C- "si"

   CAT-

_____

D- "di"

   DOG-

_____

E- "y"

   EGG-

_____

F- "ehf"

   FISH-

_____

G- "ji"

   GOAT-

_____

ROMPER LA BARRERA DEL IDIOMA INGLÉS NIVEL 1

WWW.ELPRINCIPECENTRE.COM
info@elprincipecentre.com

H - "jech"

HAT -

___

I - "ay"

IGLOO -

___

J - "jey"

JELLY -

___

K - "key"

KITE -

___

L - "el"

LEAF -

___

M - "em"

MOON -

___

N - "en"

NEST -

___

O- "oh"

ORANGE-

_____

P- "pi"

PENGUIN-

_____

Q- "kiu"

QUEEN-

_____

R- "ar"

RING-

_____

S- "es"

SUN-

_____

T- "ti"

TREE-

_____

U- "iu"

UMBRELLA-

_____

V- "vi"

VASE-

___

W- "dubelyu"

WHALE-

___

X- "ex"

X-RAY-

___

Y- "guay"

YELLOW-

___

Z- "sed"

ZEBRA-

___

 TOP TIPS!!

1. Verbos auxiliares/ Verbos ayudantes.

Cuando hacemos preguntas o negaciones en inglés usamos el verbo auxiliar "do" o "to be". También normalmente hay una forma completa de la frase y otra contactrada.
-¿ Dónde vives?- Where do you live?
-Ella no sabe la verdad- She does not/ doesn´t know the truth
-No queremos ir- We do not/ don´t want to go
-¿Dónde estudiáis?- Where do you study? /Where are you studying?/ Where´re you studying?
-No vamos alli- We do not/ don´t go there/ We are not/´re not/ aren´t going there.

TOP TIPS!!

2. QUESTION TAGS

En inglés, en vez de usar "no"/ "a que sí" / "a que no" / "verdad" al final de una pregunta, usamos un "question tag".
Sirven para confirmar que decimos o generar una respuesta de la persona con que hablamos.
Nota que en inglés no usamos "¿" para empezar una pregunta, solo "?" para terminar.

Por ejemplo:

-¿Vives en España, ¿no? - You live in Spain, **do you not/don´t you?**
-¿Eres medico, ¿no? - You are a doctor, **are you not/ aren´t you?**
-¿ Él está felíz, ¿verdad? - He is happy, **is he not/ isn´t he?**
-No queremos comprar una casa, ¿a que sí? - We don´t want to buy a house, **do we?**
- Sois los dos profesores, ¿verdad? - You are both teachers **are you not/ aren´t you?**
Trabajan duro, ¿verdad? - They do work hard, **do they not/ don´t they?**
- Tocas la guitarra, ¿a que sí? - You play the guitar, **do you not/ don´t you?**
- A Diane, le gustan los perros, ¿a que si?- Diane likes dogs, **does she not/ doesn´t she?**
- No queremos aprender chino, ¿a que no?- We don´t want to learn Chinese **do we?**

También para contestar a una pregunta podemos solo usar el auxiliar:

¿Te gustan los perros? - Do you like dogs? **Yes, I do/ No, I do not/ don´t**
¿Viven en España? – Do they live in Spain? **Yes, they do/ No, they do not/ don´t.**
¿Vamos a la fiesta? – Are we going to the party? **Yes, we are/ No, we are not/ aren´t.**

2. LOS ARTÍCULOS- DEFINDO Y INDEFINIDOS

Los sustantivos son nombres. De personas, cosas, nombre de cualquiera cosa.
En español todos los sustantivos son masculinos o femininos. Entonces los artículos que usamos dependen en el género del sustantivo. También si hablamos en singular o plural.

Definidos:
el libro (masculino/singular)   **la** casa (femenino/singular)
los libros (masculino/ plural)   **las** casas (femenino/ plural)

Indefinidos:
un libro (masculino/singular)   **una** casa (femenino/singular)
unos libros (masculino/plural)   **unas** casas (femenino/ plural)

En inglés tenemos la suerte de no tener masculino y femenino de sustantivos, ☺ entonces no hay tanto para pensar.
Definido:
Solo "**the**", singular o plural
The book, **the** house, **the** books, **the** houses- Para todos!!!!!

Indefinidos:
a, an, (sí el sustantivo empieza por vocal)- singular
some- plural
A book, **a** house, **an** apple, **some** books, **some** houses, **some** apples

PRACTICE A: SINGULAR- Busca estas palabras en inglés y pon el artículo adecuado. Practica pronunciarlas y deletrearlas.*(YOUTUBE)*

1. La oficina
2. Un/a medico/a
3. El coche
4. Una falda
5. La estrella
6. Una naranja
7. El supermercado
8. Un ordenador
9. El aeropuerto
10. El/la profesor/a
11. Un elefante

ROMPER LA BARRERA DEL IDIOMA INGLÉS NIVEL 1
WWW.ELPRINCIPECENTRE.COM
info@elprincipecentre.com

12. La revista
13. Un/a perro/a
14. La silla

PRACTICA B: PLURAL -Busca estas palabras en inglés y pon el artículo adecuado. Practica pronunciarlas y deletrearlas. (YOUTUBE)

1. Las flores
2. Unas patatas
3. Las bebidas
4. Unos edificios
5. Los bancos
6. Unas tiendas
7. Las mesas
8. Unos periódicos
9. Los teléfonos
10. Unos armarios
11. Las cocinas
12. Unos jardines
13. Las señoras
14. Unos chicos

3. NÚMEROS

PRACTICA A: Escucha la pronuncicion de estos números y practica decirlos. (YOUTUBE)

1	one	39	thirty-nine	77	seventy-seven
2	two	40	forty	78	seventy-eight
3	three	41	forty-one	79	seventy-nine
4	four	42	forty-two	80	eighty
5	five	43	forty-three	81	eighty-one
6	six	44	forty-four	82	eighty-two
7	seven	45	forty-five	83	eighty-three
8	eight	46	forty-six	84	eighty-four
9	nine	47	forty- seven	85	eighty- five
10	ten	48	forty-eight	86	eighty- six
11	eleven	49	forty-nine	87	eighty- seven
12	twelve	50	fifty	88	eighty- eight
13	thirteen	51	fifty-one	89	eighty-nine
14	fourteen	52	fifty-two	90	ninety
15	fifteen	53	fifty-three	91	ninety-one
16	sixteen	54	fifty-four	92	ninety-two
17	seventeen	55	fifty- five	93	ninety-three
18	eighteen	56	fifty- six	94	ninety-four
19	nineteen	57	fifty-seven	95	ninety- five
20	twenty	58	fifty- eight	96	ninety- six
21	twenty- one	59	fifty- nine	97	ninety- seven
22	twenty-two	60	sixty	98	ninety- eight
23	twenty-three	61	sixty-one	99	ninety-nine
24	twenty-four	62	sixty-two	100	one hundred
25	twenty-five	63	sixty-three	101	one hundred and one
26	twenty-six	64	sixty-four	102	one hundred and two
27	twenty-seven	65	sixty- five	103	one hundred and three
28	twenty-eight	66	sixty- six	104	one hundred and four(etc)
29	twenty-nine	67	sixty-seven	200	two hundred
30	thirty	68	sixty- eight	300	three hundred
31	thirty-one	69	sixty- nine	400	four hundred
32	thirty-two	70	seventy	500	five hundred
33	thirty-three	71	seventy-one	600	six hundred
34	thirty-four	72	seventy-two	700	seven hundred
35	thirty-five	73	seventy-three	800	eight hundred
36	thirty-six	74	seventy-four	900	nine hundred
37	Thirty-seven	75	Seventy-cinco	1000	one thousand
38	Thirty-eight	76	Seventy- six	1001	one thousand and one (etc)

1,000,000 – one million

4. PRACTICA LOS NÚMEROS

PRACTICA A: escribe los números y practica decirlos. (YOUTUBE)

1. 121
2. 567
3. 54
4. 1,457
5. 999
6. 632
7. 32
8. 768
9. 2,530
10. 5,324
11. 724
12. 17
13. 852
14. 15
15. 61
16. 333
17. 1,023
18. 155
19. 592
20. 431
21. 77
22. 888
23. 923
24. 67
25. 274
26. 92
27. 5,232
28. 24
29. 87
30. 165

5. ROPA Y NÚMEROS

La Ropa – Clothes
Costs (singular)/ cost (plural) - Cuesta/Cuestan (plural)

1. Los guantes – the gloves
2. La camisa – the shirt
3. La bufanda – the scarf
4. Los pantalones – the trousers
5. Los zapatos – the shoes
6. Los calcetines – the socks
7. El jersey – the jumper
8. La falda – the skirt
9. La chaqueta – the jacket
10. La camiseta – the t-shirt
11. El vestido – the dress
12. El sombrero – the hat

Preguntas y respuestas: Nota que en inglés usamos el verbo auxiliar "to do" para hacer preguntas. (ve TOP TIPS PÁGINA 7)

SINGULAR:

¿Cuánto cuesta la chaqueta? - **How much <u>does</u> the jacket cost?**

La chaqueta cuesta ………. euros - **The jacket costs** ……….

PLURAL:

¿Cuánto cuestan las zapatos? - **How much <u>do</u> the shoes cost?**

Los zapatos cuestan ………. euros- **The shoes cost** ……….

PRACTICA A: Pregunta y contesta los precios de la ropa abajo. (YOUTUBE)

1. £25.00   2. £31.99   3. £9.99   4. £15.44

 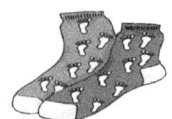  

5. £18.70   6. £9.99   7. £33.60   8. £47.20

9. £45.20   10. £33.62   11. £90.00   12. £18.71

Top Tips!!

3. Nuncas usamos el singular de "ropa/ropas"

Solo "clothes"- plural. Por ejemplo-

Compro la ropa/ las ropas en la tienda- I buy **clothes** at the shop.

"**Cloth**" significa material para hacer algo o un trapo para limpiar.

Tengo la material para hacer una falda - I have the **cloth** to make a skirt.

Limpio la mesa con un trapo mojado – I clean the table with a damp **cloth.**

6. WHAT TIME IS IT? - ¿QUE HORA ES?

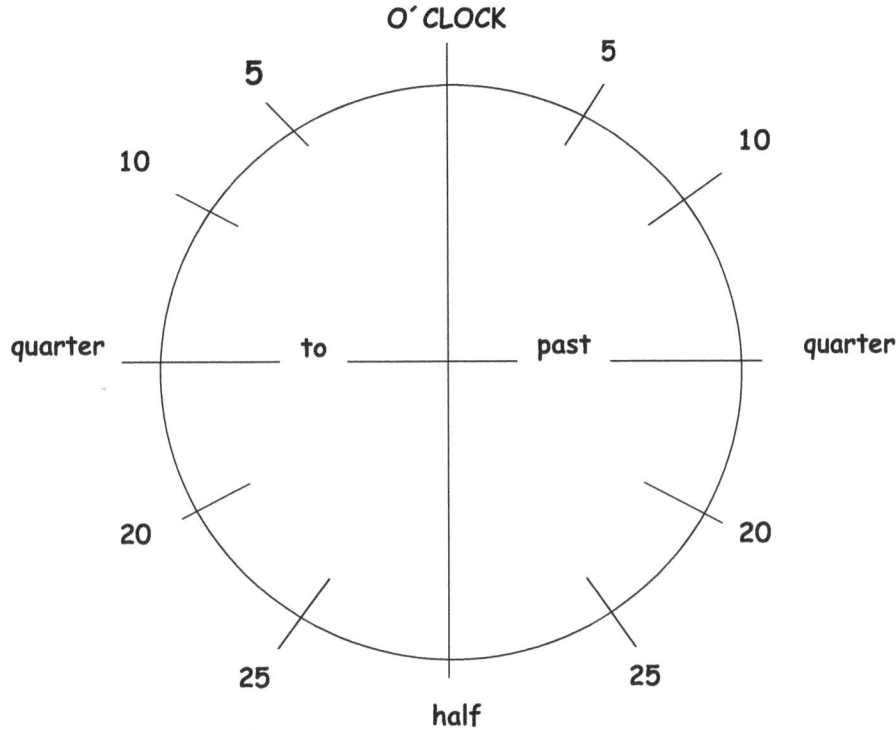

En inglés para decir ambos "son las" y "es la" usamos "It is / it´s".
Empezamos con **los minutos** primero, (si hay) no **la hora** como en español.

Por ejemplo:

a) **Son las tres en punto- It is/It´s 3 o´clock.**
b) **Son las cuatro y media- It is/It´s half past four**
Pero también se puede decir- **It is/It´s four thirty**
c) **Son las diez menos cuarto- It is/ It´s quarter to ten**
Pero también se puede decir- **It is/ It´s nine forty-five**

PRACTICA A: Escribe estas horas en las formas posibles, para algunas hay más de una/ Write out the following times in full in their possible forms, sometimes there are more than one (YOUTUBE)

1. Son las once y media
2. Son las cuatro menos cuarto

3. Es la una y diez
4. Es la una menos veinticinco
5. Son las dos en punto
6. Son las ocho y veinticinco
7. Son las nueve y veinte
8. Es la una y veinticinco
9. Son las diez y media
10. Son las nueve menos cuarto

PRACTICANDO LA HORA/ PRACTICING THE TIME

Salir - to leave   **Llegar - to arrive**   **A - at**

Ejemplo:
¿A qué hora <u>sale</u> el tren? - What time <u>does</u> the train leave? **(AUXILLIARY VERB)**
El tren <u>sale</u> a las doce - The train leaves at 12.00
¿A que hora <u>llega</u> el tren? - What time <u>does</u> the train arrive? **(AUXILLIARY VERB)**
El tren <u>llega</u> a las cuatro menos veinte - The train arrives at 3.40.
Nota que en la pregunta, en inglés no es necesario decir "a" (at)

PRACTICA B: Siguiendo el ejemplo arriba, escribe las preguntas y respuestas con las horas completas y practica decirlas/ Following the example above, write out the questions and answers with the times in full and practice saying them. (YOUTUBE)

	leaves	arrives
1. The train	10.15	8.00
2. The bus	11.10	5.30
3. The aeroplane	10.20	3.10
4. The postman	10.05	3.10
5. The doctor	8.45	9.45
6. The nurse	12.35	1.15
7. The secretary	4.45	2.30
8. The woman	5.50	6.40
9. The teacher	3.25	11.25
10. Susan	1.20	6.05

PRACTICA C: Haz el mismo usando estos verbos distintos/ Do the same using these different verbs. (YOUTUBE)

Comenzar - to begin   Terminar - to finish

For example:
¿A qué hora comienza la película? -What time does the film start?
La película comienza a las doce - The film starts at 12.00.
¿A qué hora termina la película? - What time does the film finish?
La película termina a las cuatro menos veinte - The film finishes at 3.40.

	starts	finishes
1. The match	10.15	12.15
2. The programme	4.15	5.30
3. The show	10.20	3.10
4. The exhibition	9.20	7.40
5. The singer	8.45	9.45
6. The meal	1.30	3.50
7. The party	4.45	2.30
8. The dinner	10.10	1.15
9. The class	3.25	11.05
10. The dance	11.30	4.00

7. El VERBO "TO BE" - "SER"/ "ESTAR"

En inglés solo tenemos un verbo que significa "ser" y "estar"- los dos!!
Tenemos forma completa y forma abreviada del verbo, como en el cuadro abajo.
En inglés no se puede omitir la persona y decir solo el verbo como en español, la frase no tendría sentido por que el verbo no cambia para cada persona.
Nota también que no tenemos formas plurales ni formales de "tú". ¿Facíl no?☺

SER-INFINITIVO	ESTAR-INFINITIVO	TO BE- INFINITIVE
(YO) SOY	(YO) ESTOY	I AM / I´M
(TÚ) ERES	(TÚ) ESTÁS	YOU ARE/ YOU´RE
(ÉL/ELLA) ES	(ÉL/ELLA) ESTÁS	HE/SHE/IT IS/ HE´S/ SHE´S /IT´S
(NOSOTROS/AS) SOMOS	(NOSOTROS/AS) ESTAMOS	WE ARE/ WE´RE
(VOSOTROS/AS) SOIS	(VOSOTROS/AS) ESTÁIS	YOU ARE/ YOU´RE
(ELLOS/ELLAS) SON	(ELLOS/ELLAS) ESTÁN	THEY ARE/ THEY´RE

NEGATIVE	NEGATIVO
I am not- I´m not	No soy/no estoy
You are not-you´re not	No eres/ no estás
He/she/it is not- He´s not, she´s not, it´s not	No es/ no está
We are not- we´re not	No somos/ no estamos
You are not- you´re not	No sois/ no estáis
They are not- they´re not	No son/ no están

Entonces puedo decir yo:

1. I am/ I´m Vicki.
2. I am not/ I´m not Jane.
3. I am/ I´m an English teacher.
4. I am not/ I´m not a doctor.
5. I am/ I´m English.
6. I am not/ I´m not German.
7. I am/ I´m from Manchester.
8. I am not/ I´m not from Spain.
9. I am/ I´m blonde.
10. I am not/ I´m not dark.
11. I am/ I´m awake.
12. I am not/ I´m not tired.
13. I am/ I´m happy.

14. I am not/ I´m not sad.
15. I am/ I´m healthy.
16. I am not/ I´m not ill.
17. I am/ I´m living in San Miguel de Salinas.
18. I am not/ I´m not living in England.
19. I am/ I´m comfortable.
20. I am not/ I´m not uncomfortable.

PRACTICA A: Averigua qué significan y escribe una oración similar para cada uno, pero sobre ti.

PRACTICA B: Traduce las siguientes oraciones al español usando la forma apropiada del verbo "to be" y busca cualquier palabra que no sepas en el diccionario o movíl. (YOUTUBE)

1. Somos ingleses
2. La mesa es cuadrada
3. Estoy con mi amigo
4. No estoy con mi amigo
5. ¿Eres médico?
6. ¿Sois profesores?
7. Estamos cansados.
8. Estáis contentos.
9. No es muy alta.
10. No son de España.
11. Soy Juan.
12. Pedro y Carmen están en España.
13. Estoy triste porque no estás aquí.
14. ¿Por qué no estás feliz?
15. Es camarero.
16. Soy de los estados unidos.
17. No sois mis amigos.
18. Es guapo.
19. ¿Está casado o soltero?
20. Ella está en clase y él está en jardín.
21. Estamos enfadadas.
22. El cielo no está gris.
23. Jane está divorciada.
24. El café está frio.
25. Ella no es muy interesante.

26. Son franceses de Paris.
27. Sois profesores.
28. Hoy no es martes.
29. Mis calcetines son blancos.
30. ¿Quién eres?
31. ¿Quiénes sois?
32. Jenifer Aniston es actríz.

Aprende de memoria el verbo "TO BE"!!!

I am/ I'm
You are/ you´re
He/she/it is- He´s/ she´s/ it´s
We are/ we´re
You are/ you´re
They are/ they´re

Top Tips!!

4. PALABRAS INTERROGATIVAS/ QUESTION WORDS

WHO? ---------- ¿QUIÉN?
WHAT? --------- ¿QUÉ?
WHEN? ---------¿CUÁNDO?
WHERE? -------¿DÒNDE?
WHY? ---------- ¿POR QUÉ?
WHICH? ------- ¿CUÁL?
HOW? ---------- ¿CÓMO?

8. EL VERBO "TO BE" EN CONTEXTO/ THE VERB "TO BE" IN CONTEXT- 1

PRACTICA A: PRACTICA LEER ESTA CONVERSACIÓN EN VOZ ALTA. (YOUTUBE)

CLASE DE INGLÉS/ ENGLISH CLASS

Pedro : Hello! I´m Pedro
Ana : I´m Ana.
Pedro : Pleased to meet you. I´m Spanish, from Madrid. And you Ana? Where are you from?
Ana : I´m Russian from Moscow.
Pedro : Are they also Russian?
Ana : No, they´re not Russian. Paulo is Italian, from Rome. Claudia is French, from Paris. Paco is South American, from Columbia. Who´s the English teacher?
Pedro : John Jones is the teacher.
Ana : What´s John Jones like?
Pedro : He is tall, dark and very nice.
Ana : Is he English or American?
Pedro : He´s English from London.

PRACTICA B: Encuentra todos los ejemplos del verbo "to be". Hay 16 en total. Después traducir el texto en Español. (YOUTUBE)

PRACTICA C: Traduzca estas preguntas al inglés, después contestar en inglés. (YOUTUBE)

1. ¿De dónde es Pedro?
2. ¿De dónde es Ana?
3. ¿Es Paulo italiano?
4. ¿Es Claudia alemana?
5. ¿De dónde es Paco?
6. ¿Quién es el profesor?
7. ¿Qué es John Jones?
8. ¿Cómo es John Jones?
9. ¿De dónde es John Jones?
10. ¿De dónde eres tú?

PRACTICA D: Traducción de conversación. Usando la conversación anterior como guía, traduzca esta conversación al inglés. (YOUTUBE)

JUAN : Hola, soy Juan. ¿Quién eres tú?
CARMEN: Yo soy Carmen. ¿Eres estudiante de inglés?
JUAN : No, no soy estudiante de inglés, soy estudiante de alemán. ¿y tú?
CARMEN: Soy estudiante de alemán también.
JUAN : ¿De dónde eres?
CARMEN: Soy Española de Alicante. Y tú?
JUAN: Soy español también, de Sevilla.
CARMEN: ¿Quién es el professor de alemán?
JUAN : Señora Schmidt.
CARMEN: ¿Cómo es ella y de dónde es?
JUAN : Es baja, rubia y muy simpática. Es de Munich.

PRACTICA E: Ahora traduzca estas preguntas en inglés y contestar en inglés. (YOUTUBE)

1. ¿Es Juan estudiante de inglés?
2. ¿Es Carmen estudiante de inglés?
3. ¿De dónde es Carmen?
4. ¿De dónde es Juan?
5. ¿Quién es el professor de alemán?
6. ¿Cómo es Señora Scmidt??
7. ¿Quién es tu professor de inglés?
8. ¿Cómo es?
9. ¿De dónde eres tú?
10. ¿Cómo eres tú?

9. EL VERBO "TO BE" EN CONTEXTO/ THE VERB "TO BE" IN CONTEXT- 2

IN THE CLASS/ EN LA CLASE

PRACTICA A: PRACTICA LEER ESTA CONVERSACIÓN EN VOZ ALTA. (YOUTUBE)

    Paul : Good day, Susan. How are you?
    Susan : I am fine, thanks, and you?
    Paul : I´m good also. ¿Where is your sister Carol?
    Susan : She´s not in class today, she´s at home.
    Paul : Why? Is she ill?
    Susan : Yes. She has a cold.
    Paul : Where is the house?
    Susan : It´s on Sherwood Street, number 18, on the left of the street.
    Paul : Thanks.

    (In Carol´s house)

    Paul : Hi Carol, how are you?
    Carol : I have a cold, but today I´m a little better..
    Paul : I like your house, it is very pretty.
    Carol : Yes but today it is very untidy. Is the door open? I´m cold, I´m not comfortable.
    Paul : Yes, the door is open. Now it´s closed. Are you comfortable now?
    Carol : Yes, now I am fine.

PRACTICE B. Encuentra los 20 ejemplos del verbo "to be" in este texto.

PRACTICE C: Traduzca el texto al español.

PRACTICE D: Traduzca estas preguntas al inglés, después contestar en inglés. (YOUTUBE)

1. ¿Cómo está Susan?
2. ¿Dónde está su hermana Carol?
3. ¿Está enferma?

4. ¿Dónde está la casa?
5. ¿Cómo esta Carol hoy?
6. ¿Cómo es la casa?
7. ¿Cómo está hoy?
8. ¿Está Carol comóda?
9. ¿Por qué tiene frio?
10. ¿Está cómoda ahora?
11. ¿Cómo estás tú hoy?
12. ¿Estás cómodo??

Top Tips!!

5. LA DIFERENCIA ENTRE EL PRESENTE SIMPLE Y EL PRESENTE CONTINUO

PRESENTE SIMPLE:
Usamos el presente simple para hablar de cosas que siempre hacemos. Rutinas, trabajos, hábitos, etc

-Donde trabajas? Trabajo en un banco.
Where do you work? I work in a bank.

-¿Qué hace él los domingos? Va a la iglesia.
What does he do on Sundays? He goes to church.

PRESENTE CONTINUO:
Igual que en español, lo usamos para hablar de cosas que hacemos en el momento. Pero también para un plan en el futuro cercano o acciones que no están pasando ahora mismo, pero sobre este tiempo.

-¿Que haces esta tarde? Me lavo el pelo
What are you doing this evening? I am washing my hair.

-¿Qué estudias este año? Estudio inglés.
What are you studying this year? I am/ I´m studying English

10. CONVERSACIÓN CON EL VERBO "TO BE" - CONVERSATION PRACTICE WITH THE VERB "TO BE".

PRACTICE A: Traduzca estas preguntas al inglés y contesta personalmente/ Translate these questions into Spanish and answer them personally. (YOUTUBE)

1. ¿De dónde eres?
2. ¿Dónde está tu casa?
3. ¿Cómo es tu casa?
4. ¿Cuándo es Navidad?
5. ¿Dónde está el Palacio de Buckingham?
6. ¿Por qué es inglés importante?
7. ¿Cómo es España??
8. ¿Quién es tu mejor amigo?
9. ¿Dónde está tu coche?
10. ¿Cuándo es tu cumpleaños?
11. ¿Estás cansado?
12. ¿Estás felíz?
13. ¿De qué color es tu coche?
14. ¿Cuál día es?
15. ¿Con quién estás?
16. ¿Cuál es mejor, el campo o la playa?
17. ¿Estás en casa?
18. ¿Quién es tu actor favorito?
19. ¿Cuál es tu comida favorita?
20. ¿Qué es importante en tu vida?

 Top Tips!!

6. La diferencia entre "speak" y "talk".

"Speak" es más para conversacións de solo una persona y es más formal-
I speak to him every day- Hablo con él cada día
"Talk" es más informal y implica conversación entre varios personas-
They are all talking- Todos hablan.
Nunca usamos "talk" para idiomas:
"I **speak** English" no "I **talk** English"

11. DESCRIBIENDO LA GENTE- DESCRIBING PEOPLE

¿Cómo es?   What is he/she like?
¿Cómo son?   What are they like?

No temenos plurales de descripciones en inglés ni masculino ni femenino como en español

ÉL / ELLA ES- HE IS/ SHE IS
ELLOS/ ELLAS SON- THEY ARE

alto/a/s – tall   simpático/a/s - nice   moreno/a/s - dark
bajo/a/s – short   antipático/a/s - unpleasant cantante/s - singer
guapo/a/s - good-looking   delgado/a/s – slim   actor-actor
feo/a/s – ugly   rubio/a/s – blonde   actríz - actress
gordo/a/s – fat   calvo/a – bald   político/a/s- politician
casado/a/s-married   separado/a/s-separated
soltero/a/s-single   viudo/a/s-widowed
divorciado/a/s-divorced

TIENE/TIENEN - he/she has

<u>ojos - eyes</u>   <u>pelo - hair</u>   <u>otros/ others</u>
azules – blue   rubio - blonde   hijos - children
verdes - green   moreno - dark   una barba- a beard
grises - grey   negro-black   un bigote- a moustache
castaños - brown   gris - grey   gafas- glasses
                           blanco-white
                           liso - straight
                           rizado - curly
                           largo - long
                           corto - short
                           ondulado - wavy

¿QUIÉN ES? – Who is it?

PRACTICA A: Practica leyendo estas descripciónes de personas famosas en voz alta. (YOUTUBE)

PRACTICA B: Traduzca al español y averiguar quien es/ Translate into English and guess who it is.

1. He is Spanish, and he´s around forty-five years old. He is tall and dark with brown eyes. He´s very handsome with curly brown hair. He´s a singer. His father is also a very famous Spanish singer. He is married to a famous Russian tennis player and they have three children. Two of his children are twins. Who is he?

2. She is Columbian. She is very attractive with long, wavy blonde hair. She is about forty-five years old. She isn´t married but she has two children. Her current partner is a Spanish football player and he is ten years younger than her. One of her most famous songs is in English and talks about a part of the body that doesn´t lie. She is famous all over the world. Who is she?

3. They are English. They´re married and they have 4 children, three boys and a girl. He is a retired footballer and she is a businesswoman, previously a singer in a very famous British girl group. He is blonde, slim, very handsome, and normally has a short beard and moustache. He has blue eyes. She´s very slim and has short, dark hair. She has brown eyes. They are both about forty-six years old. Who are they?

PRACTICA C: Piensa en un hombre famoso y escribe una descripción similar en inglés. Después haz el mismo sobre una mujer famosa y después más de una persona (Por ejemplo, un matrimonio, un grupo, un dúo). Entonces léelo en voz alta a alguien que hable inglés para ver si sepan quien es.

12. THERE IS/THERE ARE- HAY

En inglés para decir "hay" es una de las muy pocas occasiones que usamos singular y plural mientras en español solo hay una forma para decirlo.

Singular- **There is /Is there?**
Plural- **There are/ Are there?**
P.e :
En mi jardín <u>hay</u> una piscina - **In my garden <u>there is</u> a swimming pool.**
En el parque <u>hay</u> muchos árboles - **In the park <u>there are</u> many trees.**

Preguntas serán así:
¿<u>Hay</u> muchas personas en la fiesta? - **<u>Are there</u> many people at the party?**
¿<u>Hay</u> algo de leche en el frigorífico? - **<u>Is there</u> any milk in the fridge?**

La negación hacemos así:

No <u>hay</u> muchos árboles en mi jardín - **<u>There are not/aren´t</u> many trees in my garden**
No <u>hay</u> nadie en la casa- **<u>There is not/ isn´t</u> anyone in the house**

PRACTICA A: *Traduzca estas preguntas al inglés y contesta personalmente/ Translate these questions into Spanish and answer them personally. (YOUTUBE)*

1. ¿Cuántos dormitorios hay en tu casa?
2. ¿Hay una television en tu dormitorio?
3. ¿Hay algunas flores en tu jardín?
4. ¿Hay cuadros en tu salón?
5. ¿Hay algunas mascotas en tu casa?
6. ¿Cuántos arbóles hay en tu jardín?
7. ¿Hay algunos buenos restaurants cerca de tu casa?
8. ¿Hay muchos libros en tu casa?
9. ¿Hay un coche delante de tu casa?
10. ¿Qué hay en tu mesita de noche?

13. HAY, SER, ESTAR/ There is, there are, "to be"

PRACTICA A: Encuentra que significan estas palabras. Eschuchalos en el YOUTUBE y practica decirlas.

1. There is/There are …

    A table/some tables
    A chair/ some chairs
    A window/ some windows
    A picture/ some pictures
    A lamp/ some lamps
    A coffee table/ some coffee tables
    A rug/ some rugs
    An armchair/ some armchairs

    A magazine/ some magazines
    A newspaper/ some newspapers
    A television/ some televisions
    A book/ some books
    A light/ some lights
    A sofa/ some sofas
    A bookcase/ some bookcases
    A cupboard/ some cupboards

2. It is/ it´s/is/ They are/ They´re/ are …

    On the left/ right
    Above
    On
    On top of
    In
    In front of
    Behind
    At the side of
    High
    Low
    Long
    Rectangular
    Narrow

    In the centre of
    In the corner
    Around
    On the wall
    Under/ underneath
    Between
    Near to
    Pretty
    Square
    Round
    Big
    Small
    Wide

PRACTICA C: Usálas para describir la foto. Ház por lo menos 250 palabras. P.e. In the room there are two sofas. The sofas are in the centre of the room. Etc, etc.

14. LA CASA DE JOHN/ JOHN´S HOUSE

PRACTICA A: Escucha este texto en YouTube y practica leerlo en voz alta-Listen to this on the YOUTUBE and practice reading it out loud.

John Jones is English. He´s from Manchester. He´s a waiter. He is tall, blonde, and has grey eyes and glasses. He´s very nice. Where is he today? Today he is at home. In the house there are two bedrooms, a bathroom, a kitchen, a dining room and a living room. John is in the living room.

What is the living room like? It is very big. In the living room there is a table, a sofa, an armchair, some chairs and a television. On the floor there is a rug. A dog is sitting on the rug underneath a chair. John´s mother is sitting in an armchair. The armchair is very comfortable. Pedro is sitting on the sofa.

What is there on the table? On the table there is a cup and in the cup there is coffee. There is also a magazine and some books. On the wall there is a mirror and some pictures. The television is under the mirror.

PRACTICA B: Encuentra todos los ejemplos del verb "to be" o "there is/are"- Find all the examples of the verb "to be" or "there is/are". (23)

PRACTICA C: Traduzca al español-Translate the text into Spanish.

PRACTICA D: Traduzca las preguntas al español y contesta en español-Translate the questions below into Spanish and then answer them in Spanish. (YouTube)

1. ¿De dónde es John?
2. ¿Qué es John?
3. ¿Cómo es John?
4. ¿Dónde está hoy?
5. ¿Cuántos dormitories hay en la casa?
6. ¿Cómo es el salón?
7. ¿Qué hay en el suelo?
8. ¿Dónde está el perro?
9. ¿Dónde está la madre de John?

10. ¿Qué hay en la mesa?
11. ¿Dónde están los cuadros?
12. ¿Dónde está la televisión?

 Top Tips!!

---

7. EL VERBO "TO GO" IR- (VE PÁGINA 133)

PRESENTE SIMPLE
I go
You go
He/ she/ it goes
We go
You go
They go

PRESENTE CONTINUO
I am/ I´m going
You are/ ´re going
He/ she/ it is/ ´s going
We are/´re going
You are/´re going
They are/´re going

PREGUNTAS
-¿Adónde vas?- Where are you going?
- ¿Quién va a la playa?- Who is going to the beach?
-¿Cuándo van a la playa- When do they go to the beach?
- ¿Por qué vais al hospital? Why are you going to the hospital?

NEGATIVOS
-No voy a la playa- I do not/ don´t go/I am/ I´m not going to the beach
-Ella no va a la escuela- She does not/ doesn´t go/ is not/ isn´t going to school

15. VERBOS REGULARES "AR" REGULAR VERBS - CONJUGATION – 'AR' VERBS

Un verbo es una palabra de acción, algo que hacemos. En español, a lo mejor ya sabes que todos los verbos terminan en "ar", "er" o "ir". Todas las tres conjugaciones tined distinctas terminaciones según la persona y tiempo en que queremos hablar. En inglés no es así, es mucho más fácil.

En inglés todos los verbos en sus infinitivos empiezan por "to". "To dance- bailar" "to eat-comer" "to drink-beber" "to buy-comprar". Todos son verbos en el infinitivo, no refieren a ninguna persona ni tiempo.

Solo hay **UNA** conjugación para **TODOS** en cada tiempo, salvo los verbos irregulares. Sin embargo, para ayudar comprender poco a poco y crecer conversación en la misma manera vamos a aprender verbos útiles de los conjugaciones españoles en tres partes.

VERBOS CON "AR"
HABLAR – to speak

PERSONA	HABLAR (INFINITIVE)	TO SPEAK (INFINITIVE)
1 persona singular	(yo) hablo	I speak
2 person singular	(tú) hablas	You speak
3 person singular	(Él/ella) habla	He/she/it speaks
1 person plural	(nosotros/as) hablamos	We speak
2 person plural	(vosotros/as) habláis	You (s) speak
3 person plural	(ellos/as) hablan	They speak

Nota que en inglés solo cambia la tercera persona singular, añadimos una "s". Entonces no se puede omitir la persona como en español, o no sabríamos de quien hablemos.

Otra cosa es que muchas veces en inglés usamos el "ing" (presente continuo) con el verbo "to be", por ejemplo

Yo trabajo- puede ser:
I work
I am/I´m working.

HACIENDO PREGUNTAS Y NAGATIVOS- MAKING QUESTIONS AND NEGATIVES.

Cuándo hacemos una pregunta or negativo en inglés temenos que usar un verbo auxiliar como "to do" o "to be".
Por ejemplo:

Do you speak Spanish?- ¿Hablas español?
I do not/ don´t speak Spanish- No hablo español.
What are you waiting for? - ¿Qué esperas?
I am not/I´m not waiting- No espero.
Does he/she speak Spanish?- ¿Habla él/ella español?
He/she does not/ doesn´t speak Spanish- él/ella no habla español.
What is he/she waiting for?- ¿ A qué espera él/ ella?
They are not/aren´t waiting- No esperan.

Entonces hacer preguntas es un poco mas complicado en inglés que en español.

PRACTICA A: Todas estos verbos son regulares y tienen la misma conjugación. Encuentralas en español y conjúgelas- All the following verbs are regular 'ar' verbs and follow the same pattern. Find their meanings in your dictionary and conjugate them: (YOUTUBE)

1. To walk – andar/ caminar (Ejemplo)

POSITIVO (PRESENTE SIMPLE)	NEGATIVO
I walk	I do not/ don´t walk
You walk	You do not walk
He/she/it walks	He/she/it does not/ doesn´t walk
We walk	We do not/ don´t walk
You walk	You do not/ don´t walk
They walk	They do not/ don´t walk
POSITIVO (PRESENTE CONTINUOUS)	NEGATIVO
I am/ I´m walking	I am not/ I´m not walking
You are/you´re walking	You are not/you´re not walking
He/she/ it is/he´s/she/it´s walking	He/she/it is not/isn´t walking
We are/are´t walking	We are not/ aren´t walking
You are/you´re walking	You are not/you´re not walking
They are walking	They are not/aren´t walking

INTERROGATIVO (PRESENTE SIMPLE)
Do I/ Do I not/Don´t I walk?
Do you/ Do you not/Don´t you walk?
Does he/she/it/Does he/she/it not/Doesn´t he/she/it walk?
Do we/ Do we not/Don´t we walk?
Do you/ Do you not/Don´t you walk?
Do they/Do they not/ Don´t they walk?
INTERROGATIVO (PRESENTE CONTINUO)
Am I walking?
Are you/are you not walking?
Is he/she/it not/Isn´t he/she/it walking?
Are we not/aren´t we walking?
Are you/are you not walking?
Are they not/aren´t they walking?

2. To dance-

POSITIVO (PRESENTE SIMPLE)	NEGATIVO

POSITIVO (PRESENTE CONTINUO)	NEGATIVO

INTERROGATIVO (PRESENTE SIMPLE)

INTERROGATIVO (PRESENTE CONTINUO)

3. To look for-

POSITIVO (PRESENTE SIMPLE)	NEGATIVO

POSITIVO (PRESENTE CONTINUO)	NEGATIVO

INTERROGATIVO (PRESENTE SIMPLE)

INTERROGATIVO (PRESENTE CONTINUO)

4. To sing-

POSITIVO (PRESENTE SIMPLE)	NEGATIVO

POSITIVO (PRESENTE CONTINUO)	NEGATIVO

INTERROGATIVO (PRESENTE SIMPLE)

INTERROGATIVO (PRESENTE CONTINUO)

5. To study-

POSITIVO (PRESENTE SIMPLE)	NEGATIVO

POSITIVO (PRESENTE CONTINUO)	NEGATIVO

INTERROGATIVO (PRESENTE SIMPLE)
INTERROGATIVO (PRESENTE CONTINUO)

6. To buy-

POSITIVO (PRESENTE SIMPLE)	NEGATIVO
POSITIVO (PRESENTE CONTINUO)	**NEGATIVO**

INTERROGATIVO (PRESENTE SIMPLE)

INTERROGATIVO (PRESENTE CONTINUO)

 Top Tips!!

8. GENITIVO SAJÓN/ SAXON GENETIVE

El "genitive sajón" substituye "de" para indicar la posesión. Se usa principalmente para cosa de personas, pero también animales y entidades.
Para crearlo simplemente añadimos "´s" a un nombre.

Por ejemplo:

Es el coche de John- It is/ ´s John´s car
Es la camita de mi perro-It is/ ´s my dog´s bed
Él es el jefe de mi marido- He is/ ´s my husband´s boss
Ella es la novia de mi hijo- She is my son´s girlfriend
Es la póliza de mi empresa- It is my company´s policy
Somos los hijos del mundo- We are the world´s children
Es la cultura de España- It is Spain´s culture

7. To listen-

POSITIVO (PRESENTE SIMPLE)	NEGATIVO

POSITIVO (PRESENTE CONTINUO)	NEGATIVO

INTERROGATIVO (PRESENTE SIMPLE)

INTERROGATIVO (PRESENTE CONTINUO)

8. To wait for-

POSITIVO (PRESENTE SIMPLE)	NEGATIVO

POSITIVO (PRESENTE CONTINUO)	NEGATIVO

INTERROGATIVO (PRESENTE SIMPLE)

INTERROGATIVO (PRESENTE CONTINUO)

9. To arrive-

POSITIVO (PRESENTE SIMPLE)	NEGATIVO

POSITIVO (PRESENTE CONTINUO)	NEGATIVO

INTERROGATIVO (PRESENTE SIMPLE)

INTERROGATIVO (PRESENTE CONTINUO)

10. To look at -

POSITIVO (PRESENTE SIMPLE)	NEGATIVO
POSITIVO (PRESENTE CONTINUO)	NEGATIVO

INTERROGATIVO (PRESENTE SIMPLE)
INTERROGATIVO (PRESENTE CONTINUO)

11. To wear-

POSITIVO (PRESENTE SIMPLE)	NEGATIVO

POSITIVO (PRESENTE CONTINUO)	NEGATIVO

INTERROGATIVO (PRESENTE SIMPLE)

INTERROGATIVO (PRESENTE CONTINUO)

12. To practice-

POSITIVO (PRESENTE SIMPLE)	NEGATIVO

POSITIVO (PRESENTE CONTINUO)	NEGATIVO

INTERROGATIVO (PRESENTE SIMPLE)

INTERROGATIVO (PRESENTE CONTINUO)

13. To prepare-

POSITIVO (PRESENTE SIMPLE)	NEGATIVO

POSITIVO (PRESENTE CONTINUO)	NEGATIVO

INTERROGATIVO (PRESENTE SIMPLE)

INTERROGATIVO (PRESENTE CONTINUO)

14. To work-

POSITIVO (PRESENTE SIMPLE)	NEGATIVO

POSITIVO (PRESENTE CONTINUO)	NEGATIVO

INTERROGATIVO (PRESENTE SIMPLE)

INTERROGATIVO (PRESENTE CONTINUO)

15. To play-

POSITIVO (PRESENTE SIMPLE)	NEGATIVO

POSITIVO (PRESENTE CONTINUO)	NEGATIVO

INTERROGATIVO (PRESENTE SIMPLE)

INTERROGATIVO (PRESENTE CONTINUO)

PRACTICA B: Traduzca (cada oración usa uno de los verbos arriba)- Translate (each sentence uses one of the above verbs). (YouTube)

1. Tocan la guitarra.
2. Ella practica cada día.
3. Él prepara el contracto.
4. Chris lleva puesto pantalones y una camiseta.
5. Yo trabajo en un banco.
6. Siempre cantamos en el baño.
7. Vosotros andáis a la escuela.
8. Bailo cada sábado.
9. Ella busca su perro.
10. Nosotros estudiamos español en la escuela.
11. Yo compro carne en el supermercado.
12. Ella escucha la radio cada día.
13. Estás esperando el autobus.
14. Miro la casa.
15. Ellos llegan el viernes.

PRACTICA C: Usanda las palabras de preguntas haz preguntas para las oraciones que hiciste el ejercicio anterior- Make questions to fit the statements you did in the previous excercise. (YouTube)

Por ejemplo: 1. They play the guitar - Tocan la guitarra.

Una pregunta adecuada podría ser- A relevant question could be:
What do they play? - ¿Qué tocan?

PRACTICA D: Conversation Practice. Usando los verbos hemos aprendido, traduzca estas preguntas al inglés y contesta en inglés. (YouTube)

1. ¿Qué idiomas hablas?
2. ¿Cuándo bailas?
3. ¿Cantas karaoke?
4. ¿Dónde estudias inglés?
5. ¿Cuándo practicas inglés?
6. ¿Dónde trabajas?
7. ¿Cómo prepares una tortilla española?
8. ¿Qué música escuchas en la radio?
9. ¿Dónde compras la ropa?

10. ¿Buscas un coche nuevo?
11. ¿Qué llevas puesto?
12. ¿Andas al trabajo?
13. ¿Qué instrumentos tocas?
14. ¿Cuándo miras la tele?

 Top Tips!!

9. TOMAR- TO HAVE (VE PÁGINA 113 PARA CONJUGAR)

En inglés muchas veces usamos el verbo "to have" (tener) en vez de "to take" (tomar)
Por ejemplo:

-I have my lunch at one o´clock every day- Tomo la comida/ como/ almuerzo a las once cada día.

- I am/ I´m going to have a shower/ Voy a tomar una ducha

- Do you want to have something to eat/ drink? / Quieres tomar algo para comer/ beber?

- What are you having? / ¿Qué tomas?

I have coffee every morning/ tomo café cada mañana

I never have coffee in the evening/ Nunca tomo café por la tarde

I always have wine with my dinner/ Siempre bebo vino con la cena

I like to have noodles in a Chinese restaurant/ Me gusta tomar tallarines en un restaurant Chino

ROMPER LA BARRERA DEL IDIOMA INGLÉS NIVEL 1
WWW.ELPRINCIPECENTRE.COM
info@elprincipecentre.com

16. VERBOS DE "AR" EN CONTEXTO- "AR" VERBS IN CONTEXT

John and Susan are English but now they are in Spain. They are at Madrid University. John is studying Spanish and Susan is studying Spanish also. They study a lot and are very good students.

Susan speaks Spanish perfectly, and she also speaks French, English and a little German. She practices evey day in the University and with her friends. John speaks Spanish and English. He practices a lot with the other students and their friends.

On Saturdays, they both work. John works in a shop and Susan works in a bar. They earn money to buy clothes and food and to pay the rent. Every day they walk to the University. Their house is very close.

In the evenings, after classes, they study a little. They practice Spanish with their friends and then they watch the television at home. John prepares the dinner and Susan plays the guitar. After having dinner, they listen to the radio, and speak only in Spanish to practice more.

PRACTICA A: Escucha este texto en (YouTube) y practica leerlo en voz alta. Entonces, identifica los 29 verbos, y complete el cuadro de verbos abajo como el ejemplo-Listen to this text on the audio and practice reading it out loud. Then pick out the 30 verbs, and complete the verb table (YouTube)

VERBO	INFINITIVO	ESPAÑOL	PERSONA
1. ARE	TO BE	SER/ ESTAR	3a PERSONA PLURAL
2.			
3.			
4.			
5.			
6.			
7.			
8.			
9.			
10.			
11.			
12.			
13.			
14.			

15.			
16.			
17.			
18.			
19.			
20.			
21.			
22.			
23.			
24.			
25.			
26.			
27.			
28.			
29.			
30.			

PRACTICA B: Traduzca el texto al español- Translate the text into Spanish.

PRACTICA D: Traduzca estas preguntas al inglés y contesta en inglés-Translate these questions into English and answer in English. (YouTube)

1. ¿De dónde son John y Susan?
2. ¿Dónde están ahora?
3. ¿Qué estudia John?
4. ¿Quién estudia español también?
5. ¿Qué idiomas habla Susan también?
6. ¿Cuándo practica ella?
7. ¿Trabajan los dos?
8. ¿Quién trabaja en una tienda?
9. ¿Por qué ganan dinero?
10. ¿Cómo llegan a la Universidad?
11. ¿Cuándo miran la televisión?
12. ¿Quién prepara la cena?
13. ¿Qué intrumento toca Susan?
14. ¿Por qué solo hablan en español?

17. VERBOS REGULARES- 2ª CONJUGACIÓN- VERBOS CON "ER" / REGULAR VERBS – 2ND CONJUGATION – 'ER' VERBS

La conjugación es igual en inglés de los verbos con "ar".
Sólo cambiamos la tercera persona singular en presente simple donde añadimos un "s".
1. Por ejemplo: To eat- comer

POSITIVO (PRESENTE SIMPLE)	NEGATIVO
I eat	I do not/ don´t eat
You eat	You do not/ don´t eat
He/she/it eats	He/ she/ it do not/ doesn´t eat
We eat	We do not/ don´t eat eat
You eat	You do not/ don´t eat eat
They eat	They do not/ don´t eat eat
POSITIVO (PRESENTE CONTINUO)	NEGATIVO
I am/I´m eating	I am not/ I´m not eating
You are/ ´re eating	You are not/ ´re not eating
He/ she/it is/´s eating	He/ she/it is not/ isn´t eating
We are/ ´re eating	we are not/ ´re not eating
You are/ ´re eating	You are not/ ´re not eating
They are/ ´re eating	They are not/ ´re not eating

INTERROGATIVO (PRESENTE SIMPLE)
Do I / not/ don´t I eat?
Do you/ not/ don´t you eat?
Does he/ she/ it not/ doesn´t he/she/it eat?
Do we/ not/ don´t we eat?
Do you/ not/ don´t you eat?
Do they/ not/ don´t they eat?
INTERROGATIVO (PRESENTE CONTINUO)
Am I/ not/ aren´t I eating?
Are you/ not/ aren´t you eating?
Is he/ she/ it/ not/ isn´t he/ she/it eating?
Are we/not/ aren´t we eating?
Are you/ not/ aren´t you eating?
Are you/ not/ aren´t you eating

PRACTICA A: Encuentra estos verbs de "er" y conjúgalos en los cuadros como el ejemplo arriba- Find the meaning of these other regular 'er' verbs and conjugate them like the example above. (YouTube)

1. To drink

POSITIVO (PRESENTE SIMPLE)	NEGATIVO

POSITIVO (PRESENTE CONTINUO)	NEGATIVO

INTERROGATIVO (PRESENTE SIMPLE)

INTERROGATIVO (PRESENTE CONTINUO)

2. To learn

POSITIVO (PRESENTE SIMPLE)	NEGATIVO

POSITIVO (PRESENTE CONTINUO)	NEGATIVO

INTERROGATIVO (PRESENTE SIMPLE)

INTERROGATIVO (PRESENTE CONTINUO)

3. To believe

POSITIVO (PRESENTE SIMPLE)	NEGATIVO

POSITIVO (PRESENTE CONTINUO)	NEGATIVO

INTERROGATIVO (PRESENTE SIMPLE)

INTERROGATIVO (PRESENTE CONTINUO)

4. To sell-

POSITIVO (PRESENTE SIMPLE)	NEGATIVO

POSITIVO (PRESENTE CONTINUO)	NEGATIVO

INTERROGATIVO (PRESENTE SIMPLE)

INTERROGATIVO (PRESENTE CONTINUO)

5. To read-

POSITIVO (PRESENTE SIMPLE)	NEGATIVO

POSITIVO (PRESENTE CONTINUO)	NEGATIVO

INTERROGATIVO (PRESENTE SIMPLE)

INTERROGATIVO (PRESENTE CONTINUO)

6. To understand-

POSITIVO (PRESENTE SIMPLE)	NEGATIVO

POSITIVO (PRESENTE CONTINUO)	NEGATIVO

INTERROGATIVO (PRESENTE SIMPLE)

INTERROGATIVO (PRESENTE CONTINUO)

7. To run-

POSITIVO (PRESENTE SIMPLE)	NEGATIVO

POSITIVO (PRESENTE CONTINUO)	NEGATIVO

INTERROGATIVO (PRESENTE SIMPLE)

INTERROGATIVO (PRESENTE CONTINUO)

8. To cough-

POSITIVO (PRESENTE SIMPLE)	NEGATIVO
POSITIVO (PRESENTE CONTINUO)	NEGATIVO

INTERROGATIVO (PRESENTE SIMPLE)
INTERROGATIVO (PRESENTE CONTINUO)

9. To break-

POSITIVO (PRESENTE SIMPLE)	NEGATIVO

POSITIVO (PRESENTE CONTINUO)	NEGATIVO

INTERROGATIVO (PRESENTE SIMPLE)

INTERROGATIVO (PRESENTE CONTINUO)

10. To see-

POSITIVO (PRESENTE SIMPLE)	NEGATIVO

POSITIVO (PRESENTE CONTINUO)	NEGATIVO

INTERROGATIVO (PRESENTE SIMPLE)

INTERROGATIVO (PRESENTE CONTINUO)

PRACTICA B: *Traduzca estas oraciones al inglés- Translate these sentences into English. (YouTube)*

1. A menudo como en un restaurante inglés.
2. Bebo leche cada díaI.
3. Él no comprende ruso.
4. Nosotros leemos muchos libros.
5. Vosotros aprendéis mucho inglés en el internet.
6. Mark vende ropa en el mercadillo.
7. Mary siempre corre en el maratón.
8. Muchos Americanos comprenden español.
9. Creemos en los OVNI.
10. Siempre tosen por la mañana.
11. ¿Aprendes inglés?
12. Yo rompo algo cada día.
13. Ella ve mucho en Netflix los fines de semana.
14. Nosotros siempre bebemos cerveza en el bar
15. Vosotros coméis muchos verduras.
16. Normalmente yo vendo coches, pero en el verano vendo casas.

PRACTICA C: *Conversation Practice. Traduzca la pregunta al inglés y contesta personalmente usando los verbos-Translate these questions into English and answer personally using the verbs. (YouTube)*

1. ¿Qué ves de la ventana de tu dormitorio?
2. ¿Por qué estudias inglés?
3. ¿Comprendes los verbs ingleses?
4. ¿Qué bebes en un restaurante?
5. ¿Crees en los fantasmas?
6. ¿Vendes tu casa?
7. ¿Rompes muchas cosas?
8. ¿Lees muchos libros?
9. ¿Dónde normalmente comes los domingos?
10. ¿Tosen los fumadores más que los no fumadores?
11. ¿Comes muchas verduras?
12. ¿Cuándo bebes alcohol en la casa?
13. ¿Cuándo corres?
14. ¿Aprendes mejor por la mañana o por la noche?
15. ¿Por qué bebes agua en verano?

17. VERBOS REGULARES "ER" EN CONTEXTO- "ER" VERBS IN CONTEXT

PRACTICA A: Escucha este texto en YOUTUBE y practica leerlo env oz alta. Después encuentra los 35 verbs y completa el cuadro de verbos. Entonces traduzcalo al español- Listen to this text on the audio if you have it and practice reading it out loud. Then pick out the 35 verbs, complete the verb table and translate the text into Spanish.

John and Susan are in a Spanish restaurant in Madrid City Centre. Susan is drinking red wine and Pedro is drinking beer. Susan is reading a magazine and John is reading a newspaper. They understand a lot of the Spanish words but not all.

They learn a lot of Spanish with their Spanish friends, but they also learn a lot when they read newspapers and magazines, and when they watch television at night. They believe that English is very important for their future.

John sees an advert in the newspaper, a boy is selling a bicycle. They both believe that they need to buy this bicycle in order to do more excercise.

For starters, they both eat salad. For main course, Susan eats chicken and John eats pasta. For dessert, John eats ice cream and Susan eats apple pie. After having lunch, they both drink coffee with milk.

They finish having lunch at around four o´clock . When they pay the bill, John breaks a glass that is on the table. The waiter isn´t angry, and they both run to the bus stop because now it´s late and they need to catch the bus at quarter past four.

VERBO EN CONTEXTO	INFINITIVO	ESPAÑOL	PERSONA
1. are	To be	SER	3a P. PLURAL
2. is	To be	ESTAR	3a P. SING
3.			
4.			
5.			
6.			
7.			
8.			
9.			
10.			
11.			

12.			
13.			
14.			
15.			
16.			
17.			
18.			
19.			
20.			
21.			
22.			
23.			
24.			
25.			
26.			
27.			
28.			
29.			
30.			
31.			
32.			
33.			
34.			
35.			

PRACTICA B: Traduzca estas preguntas al inglés y contesta en inglés-Translate these questions into English and answer in English. (YouTube)

1. ¿Dónde están John y Susan?
2. ¿Qué bebe Susan?
3. ¿Quién bebe cerveza?
4. ¿Qué leen?
5. ¿Cuándo aprenden much inglés?
6. ¿Por qué creen que el español es muy importante?
7. ¿Qué ve John en el periódico?
8. ¿Qué vende el chico?
9. ¿Por qué necesitan comprar esta bicicleta?
10. ¿Qué comen las dos de primero?
11. ¿Quién come paella de segundo?
12. ¿Qué come John de postre?

13. ¿Qué beben los dos después de comer?
14. ¿A qué hora terminan de comer?
15. ¿Qué rompe John cuando pagan la cuenta?
16. ¿Está enfadado el camarero?
17. ¿Por qué corren a la parada del autobús?
18. ¿A qué hora necesitan coger el autobús?

Top Tips!!

10. PARTES DEL CUERPO/ PARTS OF THE BODY

La mano- hand
El brazo- arm
El dedo- finger
La pierna- leg
La cabeza- head
La nariz- nose
Los ojos- eyes
el pie- foot
La rodilla- knee
El tobillo- ankle
Los dedos del pie- toes
El estómogo- stomach
La espalda- back

En inglés no utilizamos artículos para partes del cuerpo, más bien pronombres posesivos (ve página 109)
Por ejemplo:
-Lávate las manos- wash your hands
-Me duelen los ojos- My eyes hurt
-Él tiene que ir al médico por la espalda- He has to go to the -doctor´s because of his back
-¿Te duele la cabeza?- Does your head hurt?
-No tenemos dolor del estómago- We don´t have a pain in our stomach

19. VERBOS REGULARES "IR" - REGULAR VERBS - 3ª CONJUGATION - 'IR' VERBS

La conjugación es igual en inglés de los verbos con "ar" Y "er".
Sólo cambiamos la tercera persona singular donde añadimos un "s".

EJEMPLO- VIVIR- TO LIVE

POSITIVO (PRESENTE SIMPLE)	NEGATIVO
I live	I do not/ don´t live
You live	You do not/ don´t live
He/she/it lives	He/she/it does not/ doesn´t live
We live	We do not/ don´t live
You live	You do not/ don´t live
They live	They do not/ don´t live
POSITIVO (PRESENTE CONTINUO)	NEGATIVO
I am/ I´m living	I am not/ I´m not living
You are/ you´re living	You are not/ aren´t living
He/she/it is/´s living	He/she/it is not/ isn´t living
We are/ we´re living	We are not/ aren´t living
You are/ you´re living	You are not/ aren´t living
They are/they´re living	They are not/ aren´t living

INTERROGATIVO (PRESENTE SIMPLE)
Do I/ not/don´t I live?
Do you/ not/don´t you live?
Does he/ she/ it not/ doesn´t he/ she/it live?
Do we/ not/don´t we live?
Do you/ not/don´t you live?
Do they/ not/don´t they live?
INTERROGATIVO (PRESENTE CONTINUO)
Am I/ not/aren´t I living
Are you not/ aren´t you living?
Is he/she/it not/isn´t he/she/it living
Are we not/ aren´t we living?
Are you not/ aren´t you living?
Are they not/ aren´t they living?

ROMPER LA BARRERA DEL IDIOMA INGLÉS NIVEL 1
WWW.ELPRINCIPECENTRE.COM
info@elprincipecentre.com

PRACTICA A: Encuentra estos verbos en español y conjúgalas en inglés- Find the meaning of these other regular 'ir' verbs and conjugate them in English (YouTube):

1. To write-

POSITIVO (PRESENTE SIMPLE)	NEGATIVO

POSITIVO (PRESENTE CONTINUO)	NEGATIVO

INTERROGATIVO (PRESENTE SIMPLE)

INTERROGATIVO (PRESENTE CONTINUO)

2. To receive-

POSITIVO (PRESENTE SIMPLE)	NEGATIVO

POSITIVO (PRESENTE CONTINUO)	NEGATIVO

INTERROGATIVO (PRESENTE SIMPLE)

INTERROGATIVO (PRESENTE CONTINUO)

3. To cover-

POSITIVO (PRESENTE SIMPLE)	NEGATIVO

POSITIVO (PRESENTE CONTINUO)	NEGATIVO

INTERROGATIVO (PRESENTE SIMPLE)

INTERROGATIVO (PRESENTE CONTINUO)

4. To get on-

POSITIVO (PRESENTE SIMPLE)	NEGATIVO

POSITIVO (PRESENTE CONTINUO)	NEGATIVO

INTERROGATIVO (PRESENTE SIMPLE)

INTERROGATIVO (PRESENTE CONTINUO)

5. To discover-

POSITIVO (PRESENTE SIMPLE)	NEGATIVO

POSITIVO (PRESENTE CONTINUO)	NEGATIVO

INTERROGATIVO (PRESENTE SIMPLE)

INTERROGATIVO (PRESENTE CONTINUO)

6. To share-

POSITIVO (PRESENTE SIMPLE)	NEGATIVO

POSITIVO (PRESENTE CONTINUO)	NEGATIVO

INTERROGATIVO (PRESENTE SIMPLE)

INTERROGATIVO (PRESENTE CONTINUO)

7. To suffer -

POSITIVO (PRESENTE SIMPLE)	NEGATIVO

POSITIVO (PRESENTE CONTINUO)	NEGATIVO

INTERROGATIVO (PRESENTE SIMPLE)

INTERROGATIVO (PRESENTE CONTINUO)

8. To hand out-

POSITIVO (PRESENTE SIMPLE)	NEGATIVO

POSITIVO (PRESENTE CONTINUO)	NEGATIVO

INTERROGATIVO (PRESENTE SIMPLE)

INTERROGATIVO (PRESENTE CONTINUO)

9. To open-

POSITIVO (PRESENTE SIMPLE)	NEGATIVO

POSITIVO (PRESENTE CONTINUO)	NEGATIVO

INTERROGATIVO (PRESENTE SIMPLE)

INTERROGATIVO (PRESENTE CONTINUO)

10. To argue-

POSITIVO (PRESENTE SIMPLE)	NEGATIVO
POSITIVO (PRESENTE CONTINUO)	NEGATIVO

INTERROGATIVO (PRESENTE SIMPLE)
INTERROGATIVO (PRESENTE CONTINUO)

PRACTICA B: Traduzca al inglés-Translate (YouTube)

1. ¿Escribes muchos correos electrónicos??
2. En África, muchos niños sufren.
3. La nieve cubre las montañas.
4. Subo el tren en Barcelona.
5. Siempre descubrimos la verdad al final.
6. El profesor reparte los examenes.
7. Jack y Peter comparten un piso en Madrid.
8. ¿Recibís muchas cartas?
9. Siempre abre la Puerta para mí.
10. Discuten cada sábado noche.
11. No viven en Madrid?
12. ¿Escribes en inglés o español?
13. ¿Abre ella la tienda?
14. El cartero reparte el correo.
15. ¿No subimos el tren en Alicante?
16. No discutimos, solo hablamos.
17. Comparto todo con mi familia.
18. ¿A qué hora subo en el tren?
19. No cubrimos los muebles del jardín.
20. ¿Cuándo descubres la verdad?
21. Sufro mucho por malos vecinos.
22. Ella no recibe correo.
23. ¿El mantel cubre la mesa?
24. Fran discute con ella de nuevo.
25. No abren hasta el 4 de junio.

20. TRADUCCIÓN DE ESPAÑOL AL ESPAÑOL- VERBOS REGULARES- TRANSLATION FROM ENGLISH TO SPANISH - REGULAR VERBS

PRACTICA A: Identifica los 17 verbos en este texto- Identify the 17 verbs in this text.
Practica leerlo en voz alta (YouTube)- Practice reading it out loud.

Mark vive en Manchester con su familia. Trabaja en una tienda, y los miércoles por la tarde estudia español en una escuela privada. Mira la tele los lunes y los martes habla con sus amigos ingleses. No comprende todo.

Los jueves lee libros de historia, y los viernes visita un bar local. Siempre bebe cerveza y come pescado y patatas fritas.

Los sábados vende ropa en el mercadillo, y los domingos escribe correos electrónicos a sus amigos españoles. Aprende mucho español con ellos.

Mark es alto, moreno, y tiene ojos castaños. Es muy simpático y comparte todo con su familia.

PRACTICA B: Traduzca el texto al inglés/ Translate the text into English.

PRACTICA C: Ahora traduzca estas preguntas al inglés y contesta en inglés- Now translate the following questions into English and answer them in English. (YouTube)

1. ¿Dónde vive Mark y con quién?
2. ¿Dónde trabaja?
3. ¿Qué estudia los miércoles por la tarde?
4. ¿Dónde estudia?
5. ¿Qué hace los lunes?
6. ¿Con quién habla los martes?
7. ¿Comprende todo?
8. ¿Qué lee los jueves?
9. ¿Qué siempre come y bebe en su bar local los viernes?
10. ¿Qué vende en el mercadillo los sábados?
11. ¿A quién escribe los domingos?
12. ¿Cómo es Mark?

21. ADVERBIOS DE FRECUENCIA- ADVERBS OF FREQUENCY

PRACTICA A: Encuentra como decir estos adverbios de frecuencia en inglés- Find out how to say these adverbs of frequency in English. (YouTube)

1. SIEMPRE
2. A MENUDO
3. NORMALMENTE
4. A VECES
5. CASI NUNCA
6. NUNCA
7. DE VEZ EN CUANDO
8. UNA VEZ A LA SEMANA
9. UNA VEZ AL MES
10. UNA VEZ AL AÑO
11. CADA DÍA
12. CADA SEMANA
13. CADA MES
14. CADA SÁBADO
15. CADA MAÑANA
16. CADA TARDE

PRACTICA B: Ahora escribe una oración en inglés usando los verbos que has aprendido para cada adverbio de frecuencia-Now write a sentence in English using the verbs you have learnt so far for each adverb of frequency.

Por ejemplo: I often eat chocolate- A menudo como chocolate.
I never drink tea in the morning- Nunca bebo té por la mañana.

22. PRACTICAR VERBOS REGULARES- PRACTICE OF REGULAR VERBS

PRACTICA A: Escucha este texto en YouTube y practica leerlo en voz alta.

My name is Paul Smith. We live in Manchester, at number 6 Barlow Terrace. My father works in a bank and my mother works in a hospital. They work from Monday to Friday. My father leaves the house at 8 a.m and my mother at 9 a.m. My father catches the bus and my mother catches the train.

I study Spanish at the University. I never come home at midday, I have lunch in the dining room at the campus with my classmates. My parents have lunch at work.

My sister doesn´t work until the evening. She tidies the house, prepares the meals, washes the clothes or irons. We help with all this at weekends and she rests.

We return home at 5 or 6 p.m. My father reads the paper, my mother watches the television or reads a book. My sister sings in a bar near to the house and doesn´t have dinner with us. Often, after having dinner, I study until midnight. My parents watch the television, listen to the radio or prepare things for the morning.

PRACTICA B: Identifica los 30 verbos y pónlos en el cuadro abajo como los dos ejemplos- Find the 30 verbs in this text. Then copy them into the verb recognition table below like the two examples.

	VERBO IN CONTEXTO	INFINITIVO	ESPAÑOL	CONTEXTO	PERSONA
1	is	To be	ser	is	3a p. singular
2	We live	To live	vivir	we live	1a p. plural
3					
4					
5					
6					
7					
8					
9					
10					
11					
12					
13					
14					
15					

16				
17				
18				
19				
20				
21				
22				
23				
24				
25				
26				
27				
28				
29				
30				

PRACTICA C: Traduzca el texto al español- Translate the text into Spanish.

PRACTICA D: Traduzca estas preguntas al inglés y contesta en inglés usando el texto- Translate the following questions into English and then answer in English.

1. ¿Dónde vive Paul Smith y su familia?
2. ¿Dónde trabaja su madre y padre?
3. ¿Qué días trabajan?
4. ¿A que hora salen de la casa?
5. ¿Qué coge el padre?
6. ¿Y su madre?
7. ¿Trabaja Paul?
8. ¿Qué estudia?
9. ¿Dónde estudia?
10. ¿Vuelve a casa a mediodía?
11. ¿Dónde come?
12. ¿Dónde come sus padres?
13. ¿Trabaja su hermana?
14. ¿Qué hace en la casa?
15. ¿A qué hora vuelven a casa?
16. ¿Qué hace su madre y padre entonces?
17. ¿Dónde canta su hermana?
18. ¿Cena con ellos?
19. ¿Qué hace Paul después?
20. ¿Qué hacen sus padres?

23. DIPTONGOS-DIPTHONGS

Diptóngos no existen en inglés, pero vamos a comparar algunos por que son verbos communes en los dos idiomas- Dipthongs don´t exist in English, but we are going to compare some as they are common verbs in both languages.

DIPTONGOS 1. Primer grupo- **o** cambia a **ue**- The first group are verbs that change from **o** to **ue**.

P.e. contar - to count.

Desde ahora todas las instrucciones en inglés!

POSITIVO (PRESENTE SIMPLE)	NEGATIVO
I count	I do not/ don´t count
You count	You do not/ don´t count
He/ she/it counts	He/she/ it does not/ doesn´t count
We count	We do not/ don´t count
You count	You do not/ don´t count
They count	They do not/ don´t count
POSITIVO (PRESENTE CONTINUO)	NEGATIVO
I am/ I´m counting	I am/ I´m not counting
You are/´re counting	You are/ ´re not counting
He/ she/it is/ ´s counting	He is/ not/ isn´t counting
We are/´re counting	We are/ ´re not counting
You are/´re counting	You are/ ´re not counting
They are/´re counting	They are/ ´re not counting

INTERROGATIVO (PRESENTE SIMPLE)
Do I not/ don´t I count?
Do you not/ don´t you count?
Does He/ she/it not/ doesn´t he/ she/ it count?
Do we not/ don´t we count
Do you not/ don´t you count?
Do they not/ don´t they count
INTERROGATIVO (PRESENTE CONTINUO)
Am I/ not/ aren´t I counting?
Are you/ not/ aren´t you counting?
Is he/ she/ it/ not/ isn´t he/ she/ it counting?
Are we/ not/ aren´t we counting?
Are you/ not/ aren´t you counting?
Are they/ not/ aren´t they counting?

PRACTICE A: Find the Spanish meaning of the following dipthong o-ue verbs and conjugate them in English in the present tense: positive, negative and interrogative like the example above. (YouTube)

1. To sleep-

POSITIVO (PRESENTE SIMPLE)	NEGATIVO

POSITIVO (PRESENTE CONTINUO)	NEGATIVO

INTERROGATIVO (PRESENTE SIMPLE)

INTERROGATIVO (PRESENTE CONTINUO)

2. To cost-

POSITIVO (PRESENTE SIMPLE)	NEGATIVO
POSITIVO (PRESENTE CONTINUO)	**NEGATIVO**

INTERROGATIVO (PRESENTE SIMPLE)
INTERROGATIVO (PRESENTE CONTINUO)

3. To find-

POSITIVO (PRESENTE SIMPLE)	NEGATIVO

POSITIVO (PRESENTE CONTINUO)	NEGATIVO

INTERROGATIVO (PRESENTE SIMPLE)

INTERROGATIVO (PRESENTE CONTINUO)

4. To be able, "can"-

POSITIVO (PRESENTE SIMPLE)	NEGATIVO

POSITIVO (PRESENTE CONTINUO)	NEGATIVO

INTERROGATIVO (PRESENTE SIMPLE)

INTERROGATIVO (PRESENTE CONTINUO)

5. To return-

POSITIVO (PRESENTE SIMPLE)	NEGATIVO

POSITIVO (PRESENTE CONTINUO)	NEGATIVO

INTERROGATIVO (PRESENTE SIMPLE)

INTERROGATIVO (PRESENTE CONTINUO)

6. To remember-

POSITIVO (PRESENTE SIMPLE)	NEGATIVO

POSITIVO (PRESENTE CONTINUO)	NEGATIVO

INTERROGATIVO (PRESENTE SIMPLE)

INTERROGATIVO (PRESENTE CONTINUO)

PRACTICE B: Translate the following into English. (YouTube)

1. Duermo muy bien en España.
2. ¿Recuerdas esta cancion?
3. Vuelven el viernes.
4. No dormimos tarde.
5. Podemos abrir la puerta.
6. Ella encuentra muchas cosas en su taxi.
7. Los zapatos cuestan veinte euros.
8. Él no duerme por la noche.
9. No puedo comer mariscos.
10. ¿Puedes trabajar por mí?
11. ¿Duermen en el avión?
12. ¿Cuándo vuelves?
13. Lo recordamos muy bien.
14. ¿Cómo encuentras el curso?
15. ¿Cuánto cuesta la casa?
16. El coche no cuesta mucho.
17. No recuerdo nada.
18. No lo encuentro difícil.
19. No vuelves hasta lunes.
20. Recordáis todo.

DIPTHONGS 2. The second group are verbs that change from **e** to **ie**.
E.g cerrar- to close

POSITIVO (PRESENTE SIMPLE)	NEGATIVO
I close	I do not/ don´t close
You close	You do not/ don´t close
He/ she/it closes	He/ she/ it does not/ doesn´t close
We close	We do not/ don´t close
You close	You do not/ don´t close
They close	They do not/ don´t close
POSITIVO (PRESENTE CONTINUO)	**NEGATIVO**
I am/ I´m closing	I am not/ I´m not closing
You are/ you´re closing	You are not/ aren´t closing
He/ she/ it is/ ´s closing	He/ she/ it is not/ isn´t closing
We are/ we´re closing	We are not/ aren´t closing
You are/ you´re closing	You are not/ aren´t closing
They are/ they´re closing	They are not/ aren´t closing

INTERROGATIVO (PRESENTE SIMPLE)
Do I/ not/ don´t I close?
Do you/ not/ don´t you close?
Does he/ she/ it/ not/ doesn´t he/ she/ it close?
Do we/ not/ don´t we close?
Do you/ not/ don´t you close?
Do they/ not/ don´t they close?
INTERROGATIVO (PRESENTE CONTINUO)
Am I/ not/ aren´t I closing?
Are you/ not/ aren´t you closing?
Is he/ she/ it/ not/ isn´t he/ she/ it closing?
Are we/ not/ aren´t we closing?
Are you/ not/ aren´t you closing?
Are they/ not/ aren´t they closing?

PRACTICE C: Find the Spanish meaning of the following verbs and conjugate them like the above. (YouTube)

1. To lose-

POSITIVO (PRESENTE SIMPLE)	NEGATIVO

POSITIVO (PRESENTE CONTINUO)	NEGATIVO

INTERROGATIVO (PRESENTE SIMPLE)

INTERROGATIVO (PRESENTE CONTINUO)

2. To start-

POSITIVO (PRESENTE SIMPLE)	NEGATIVO

POSITIVO (PRESENTE CONTINUO)	NEGATIVO

INTERROGATIVO (PRESENTE SIMPLE)

INTERROGATIVO (PRESENTE CONTINUO)

3. To understand-

POSITIVO (PRESENTE SIMPLE)	NEGATIVO

POSITIVO (PRESENTE CONTINUO)	NEGATIVO

INTERROGATIVO (PRESENTE SIMPLE)

INTERROGATIVO (PRESENTE CONTINUO)

4. To prefer-

POSITIVO (PRESENTE SIMPLE)	NEGATIVO

POSITIVO (PRESENTE CONTINUO)	NEGATIVO

INTERROGATIVO (PRESENTE SIMPLE)

INTERROGATIVO (PRESENTE CONTINUO)

5. To think-

POSITIVO (PRESENTE SIMPLE)	NEGATIVO

POSITIVO (PRESENTE CONTINUO)	NEGATIVO

INTERROGATIVO (PRESENTE SIMPLE)

INTERROGATIVO (PRESENTE CONTINUO)

6. To want-

POSITIVO (PRESENTE SIMPLE)	NEGATIVO

POSITIVO (PRESENTE CONTINUO)	NEGATIVO

INTERROGATIVO (PRESENTE SIMPLE)

INTERROGATIVO (PRESENTE CONTINUO)

PRACTICE D: Translate the following into English. (YouTube)

1. La pelicula comienza/ empieza a las 9:00.
2. ¿Entiendes los verbos en ingles?
3. Él prefiere vino tinto.
4. ¿En qué piensas?
5. El partido no empieza hasta las seis de la tarde.
6. Siempre perdemos nuestras gafas de sol.
7. Quieren una casa en Inglaterra.
8. No quiero aprender alemán, quiero aprender inglés.
9. ¿Cuál coche prefieres?
10. ¿A qué hora comienza la clase?
11. No entiendo a la gente mala.
12. Entendemos todo.
13. No pensáis mal.
14. ¿Qué cosas pierdes en la casa?
15. ¿Cuál idioma quieres aprender?
16. Pensáis que España es muy bonita.
17. Ella entiende Chino muy bien.
18. Él quiere paella para comer.
19. No queremos hablar contigo.
20. Prefiero tomar pollo.

DIPTHONGS 3. With the third and last group of the stem-changing verbs, the **e** changes to **i**. These are only 'ir' verbs.

E.g repetir- to repeat:

POSITIVO (PRESENTE SIMPLE)	NEGATIVO
I repeat	I do not/ don´t repeat
You repeat	You do not/ don´t repeat
He/ she/ it repeats	He/ she/ it does not/ doesn´t repeat
We repeat	We do not/ don´t repeat
You repeat	You do not/ don´t repeat
They repeat	They do not/ don´t repeat
POSITIVO (PRESENTE CONTINUO)	NEGATIVO
I am/ I´m repeating	I am/ I´m not repeating
You are/ ´re repeating	You are/´re not repeating
He/ she/ it is/ ´s repeating	He/ she/ it is not/ isn´t repeating
We are/ ´re repeating	We are/´re not repeating
You are/ ´re repeating	You are/´re not repeating
They are/ ´re repeating	They are/´re not repeating

INTERROGATIVO (PRESENTE SIMPLE)
Do I/ not/ don´t I repeat?
Do you/ not/ don´t you repeat?
Does he/ she/ it not/ doesn´t he/ she/ it repeat?
Do we/ not/ don´t we repeat?
Do you/ not/ don´t you repeat?
Do they/ not/ don´t they repeat?
INTERROGATIVO (PRESENTE CONTINUO)
Am I/not/ aren´t I repeating?
Are you/ not/ aren´t you repeating?
Is he/ she/it / not/ isn´t he/ she/ it repeating?
Are we/ not/ aren´t we repeating?
Are you/ not/ aren´t you repeating?
Are they/ not/ aren´t they repeating?

PRACTICE E: Find the Spanish meaning of the following verbs and conjugate them in English. (YouTube)

1. To get-

POSITIVO (PRESENTE SIMPLE)	NEGATIVO

POSITIVO (PRESENTE CONTINUO)	NEGATIVO

INTERROGATIVO (PRESENTE SIMPLE)

INTERROGATIVO (PRESENTE CONTINUO)

2. To fry-

POSITIVO (PRESENTE SIMPLE)	NEGATIVO

POSITIVO (PRESENTE CONTINUO)	NEGATIVO

INTERROGATIVO (PRESENTE SIMPLE)

INTERROGATIVO (PRESENTE CONTINUO)

3. To ask for/ order/ request-

POSITIVO (PRESENTE SIMPLE)	NEGATIVO

POSITIVO (PRESENTE CONTINUO)	NEGATIVO

INTERROGATIVO (PRESENTE SIMPLE)

INTERROGATIVO (PRESENTE CONTINUO)

4. To serve-

POSITIVO (PRESENTE SIMPLE)	NEGATIVO

POSITIVO (PRESENTE CONTINUO)	NEGATIVO

INTERROGATIVO (PRESENTE SIMPLE)

INTERROGATIVO (PRESENTE CONTINUO)

5. To measure-

POSITIVO (PRESENTE SIMPLE)	NEGATIVO

POSITIVO (PRESENTE CONTINUO)	NEGATIVO

INTERROGATIVO (PRESENTE SIMPLE)

INTERROGATIVO (PRESENTE CONTINUO)

6. To follow-

POSITIVO (PRESENTE SIMPLE)	NEGATIVO

POSITIVO (PRESENTE CONTINUO)	NEGATIVO

INTERROGATIVO (PRESENTE SIMPLE)

INTERROGATIVO (PRESENTE CONTINUO)

PRACTICE F: Translate the following into English. (YouTube)

1. No frío mucha comida.
2. ¿Qué pides para beber con una paella?
3. Ella nunca sirve vino con la cena.
4. ¿Cómo puedes conseguir un buen trabajo?

5. Medimos las cortinas.
6. ¿Me seguís?
7. Él no sigue el curso muy bien.
8. No pido nada de ti.
9. ¿Qué sirven para el desayuno?
10. Ella frie una hamburguesa cada sábado.
11. ¿Qué mides?
12. Ahora es buen tiempo para conseguir un beso.
13. ¿Fries huevos con el desayuno?
14. No mido el agua que bebo.
15. El camarero sirve las bebidas en la terraza.
16. Siempre piden una cerveza en el bar.
17. Conseguimos un trabajo.
18. Sigues el coche amarillo.
19. ¿Por qué pides tanto?
20. No freimos nada.

TOP TIPS!!

---

11. PRONOMBRES POSESIVOS- POSSESSIVE PRONOUNS

No temenos plurales ni masculino/ femenino menos 3ª persona singular ☺

Mi/ mis- my
Tu/ tus- your
Su/ sus (de él o ella) - his (de él) / her (de ella)
Nuestro/a/as/as- our
Vuestro/a/os/as- your
Su/ sus (de ellos)- their

It´s my house- Es mi casa
Are they your shoes?- ¿Son tus zapatos?
They are not/ aren´t my friends- No son mis amigos
She is our cleaner- Ella es nuestra limpiadora
This is my book- Este es mi libro

PRACTICE G: Conversation Practice - Dipthongs. Translate these questions into English and reply in English. (YouTube)

1. ¿Qué normalmente pides en un restaurante chino?
2. ¿A qué hora comienzas a trabajar?
3. ¿Duermes bien en las casas de otra gente/otras personas?
4. ¿Cuánto cuesta una botella de leche en España?
5. ¿Cómo encuentras un buen mecánico en España?
6. ¿A qué hora comienzas a mirar la televisión?
7. ¿Entiendes mucho francés?
8. ¿Pierdes muchas cosas en la casa?
9. ¿Prefieres vino tinto, blanco o rosado?
10. ¿A quién recuerdas más del colegio/de la escuela?
11. ¿Vuelves a menudo a tu pueblo?
12. ¿Puedes ver el mar de tu casa?
13. ¿Piensas que Inglaterra es mejor que tu país?
14. ¿Por qué quieres hablar inglés?
15. ¿Cómo consigues un trabajo bueno en España?
16. ¿Qué normalmente sirven para el desayuno en un restaurante español?
17. ¿Fries mucha comida?
18. ¿Sigues este curso?
19. ¿Cuesta mucho comer en un restaurante en tu barrio?
20. ¿Prefieres tomar café en casa o en un bar?
21. ¿Cuentas las calorías que tomas cada día?
22. ¿Entiendes por que es importante aprender inglés?

23. DIPTHONGS -PRACTICE IN CONTEXT

PRACTICE A: Identify the 32 verbs in this text and use them to complete the verb identification table. The first 3 verbs have been done for you.

Pedro Martínez es mecánico y vive en Alicante. No recuerdo exactamente donde, pero recuerdo que su casa está cerca de la playa. Cada/ todos los viernes, va al bar y pide un menú del día que el camarero sirve en la terraza.

Vuelve a su casa después de comer a las 5, y a las 8 llega su novia Carmen. Piensan en su futuro y cuentan el dinero que tienen para comprar una casa. La casa que quieren cuesta 130 mil euros, tienen 100 mil y necesitan más. No duermen por la noche porque piensan en como pueden conseguir bastante dinero para comprar la casa.

Después de cenar, Pedro lava/friega los platos y Carmen comienza a leer el periódico. Los dos comprenden que para conseguir el dinero para la casa no pueden salir por la tarde.

	VERB	INFINITIVE	ENGLISH	PERSON
1	es	ser	To be	3rd person singular
2	vive	vivir	To live	3rd person singular
3	no recuerdo	to remember	recordar (dipthong)	1st person singular
4				
5				
6				
7				
8				
9				
10				
11				
12				
13				
14				
15				
16				
17				
18				

19			
20			
21			
22			
23			
24			
25			
26			
27			
28			
29			
30			
31			
32			

PRACTICE B: Translate the text into English. (YouTube)

PRACTICE C: Translate these questions into English and answer them in English. (YouTube)

1. ¿Qué hace Pedro?
2. ¿Dónde vive?
3. ¿Recuerdo exactamente donde está su casa?
4. ¿Adónde va cada/todos los viernes?
5. ¿Qué pide?
6. ¿Dónde sirve el camarero la comida?
7. ¿A qué hora vuelve a su casa?
8. ¿A qué hora llega su novia Carmen?
9. ¿En qué piensan?.
10. ¿Qué cuentan?
11. ¿Cuánto cuesta la casa que quieren?
12. ¿Cuánto tienen?
13. ¿Por qué no pueden dormir por la noche?
14. ¿Qué hace Pedro después de cenar?
15. ¿Qué hace Carmen?
16. ¿Qué comprenden los dos?

25. TO HAVE/ HAVE GOT- TENER

En inglés para el verbo "tener" podemos usar "to have" o "to have got".

Sin embargo, hay muchas veces en español cuando usamos "tener" pero en inglés no, más vale el verbo "to be" (ser/estar) Por ejemplo:

La edad - I am 30 years old- **NO** I have thirty years.

Estados- I am hungry/ I am tired/ I am scared- **NO** I have hunger, I have sleep, I have fear. Pero si, lo usamos para obligación como en español "tener que". En esta lección miramos como lo usamos comparandolo con el español.

1. To have

POSITIVO (PRESENTE SIMPLE)	NEGATIVO
I have	I do not/ don´t have
You have	You do not/ don´t have
He/ she/it has	He/she/it does not/ doesn´t have
We have	We do not/ don´t have
You have	You do not/ don´t have
They have	They do not/ don´t have
POSITIVO (PRESENTE CONTINUO)	NEGATIVO
I am/ I´m having	I am/ I´m not having
You are/´re having	You are/´re/ not/ aren´t having
He/ she/ it/´s having	He/she/it is/ ´s not/ isn´t having
We are/´re having	We are/´re/ not/ aren´t having
You are/´re having	You are/´re/ not/ aren´t having
They are/´re having	They are/´re/ not/ aren´t having

INTERROGATIVO (PRESENTE SIMPLE)
Do I /not/ don´t I have?
Do you/ not/ don´t you have?
Does he/ she/ it/ not/ doesn´t he/ she/ it have?
Do we/ not/ don´t we have?
Do you/ not/ don´t you have?
Do they/ not/ don´t they have?
INTERROGATIVO (PRESENTE CONTINUO)
Am I/ not/ aren´t I having?
Are you /not/ aren´t you having
Is he/she/ it/ not/ isn´t he/she/it having?
Are you /not/ aren´t you having?
Are you /not/ aren´t you having?
Are you /not/ aren´t you having?

2. To have got (no lo usamos en continuo)

POSITIVO (PRESENTE SIMPLE)	NEGATIVO
I have/´ve got	I have not / haven´t got
You have/ ´ve got	You have not / haven´t got
He/ she/ it has/´s got	He/ she/ it has not/ hasn´t got
We have/ ´ve got	I have not / haven´t got
You have/ ´ve got	You have not / haven´t got
They have/ ´ve got	They have not / haven´t got

INTERROGATIVO (PRESENTE SIMPLE)
Have I/ have I not/ haven´t I got?
Have you/ have you not/ haven´t you got?
Has he/she/it not/ hasn´t he/ she/ it got?
Have we/ have we not/ haven´t we got?
Have you/ have you not/ haven´t you got?
Have they/ have they not/ haven´t they got?

PRACTICA A- **POSSESSION:** Sobre todo, es el verbo que usamos para hablar de posesión, lo que tenemos.

Para practicar, piensa en 10 cosas que TIENES-

1. I have/ I have got/ I´ve got a/ an/ some …

2.

3.

4.

5.

6.

7.

8.

9.

10.

Después, 5 cosas que NO tienes-

1. I do not have/ don´t have/ haven´t got a/ an / any ….

2.

3.

4.

5.

6.

7.

8.

9.

10.

PRACTICE B: Translate to English. (YouTube)

1. Tengo diez euros.
2. ¿Tienes mis libros?
3. Ella tiene un coche nuevo.
4. ¿Tiene él las tazas?
5. No tenenos una casa
6. Tenéis muchos amigos.
7. Tienen cinco primos.
8. Tengo el dinero.
9. No tengo un gato.
10. ¿Quién tiene las llaves?
11. ¿Por qué no tiene ella tiempo?
12. No tienen un jardín.
13. No tienes coche grande.
14. ¿Tenéis una pregunta?
15. ¿Quién tiene la respuesta?
16. ¿Tenemos algo en el frigórifico?
17. No tengo mucho tiempo.
18. Él no tiene hermanos.
19. ¿Qué vino tienes?
20. Tengo dos perros.

EDAD/ AGE: En inglés, usamos el verbo "to be" para hablar de edad. Por ejemplo:

Tengo 50 años - I am 50 (years old).
Juan tiene 15 años - Juan is 15 (years old).
La casa tiene 7 años - The house is 7 (years old).
¿Cuàntos años tienes? - How old are you? (no usamos "years old" con interrogatives).

PRACTICE C: Translate the following into English. (YouTube)

1. Tienes treinta años.
2. Mary tiene cuarenta y cinco años.
3. Mi coche tiene diez años.
4. ¿Cuántos años tiene tu hermano?
5. Esos chicos tienen quince años

6. Su gato tiene ocho años.
7. ¿Cuántos años tienen?
8. El pueblo tiene doscientos años.
9. Tenéis menos años que yo.
10. Él tiene más años que ella.

IDIOMATIC EXPRESSIONS: There are several phrases in Spanish where we use "tener" when in English we use the verb "to be".

Tener hambre - to be hungry
Tener sed - to be thirsty
Tener frio - to be cold
Tener calor -to be hot
Tener miedo - to be afraid
Tener suerte - to be lucky
Tener prisa - to be in a hurry
Tener sueño - to be sleepy
Tener razón - to be right

PRACTICE D: Contesta la pregunta como el ejemplo- Answer the questions, like the example. (YouTube)

1. Why are you eating a sandwich? – Because I am/I´m hungry
2. Why is Juan buying a bottle of water?
3. Why do they want to sleep?
4. Why are you buying a scarf?
5. Why do I win a million pounds on the lottery?
6. Why do you agree with me?
7. Why are you hurrying?
8. Why are they hiding under the bed?
9. Why don´t you agree with her?
10. Why are you sitting in the shade?

OBLIGACIÓN: Para hablar de algo que "tenenos que" hacer usamos "to have" plus "to" plus infinitive- To talk about something we "have to" do, we use the appropriate form of the verb "to have" followed by "to" followed by the infinitve of what we have to do. For example:

Tengo <u>que</u> hablar con Juan - I have to speak to Juan.
Tienes <u>que</u> comer verduras - You have to eat vegetables.
Tienen <u>que</u> trabajar mucho - They have to work hard.

PRACTICE E: Translate the following into English. (YouTube)

1. Tengo que leer este libro?
2. Tienes que ver esta película.
3. Tenemos que lavar el coche cada sábado.
4. Ella tiene que abrir la ventana cada mañana.
5. Tenemos que decidir ahora.
6. Tenéis que vender vuestro coche.
7. No tienen que comer el desayuno.
8. Tienes que llevar el perro al parque.
9. Tenemos que comprar vino para la fiesta.
10. No tienes que esperar aquí.

26. VERBOS "GO-GO"

Cuando apredemos español llamamos estos verbos "go-go" porque en primera persona singular terminan en "go" pero después no-

P.e. salir- to leave/go out. *NB: Algunos verbos "go-go" son también diptongos, p.e tener o venir.*

POSITIVO (PRESENTE SIMPLE)	NEGATIVO
I leave	I do not/ don´t leave
You leave	You do not/ don´t leave
He/ she/ it leaves	He/ she/ it does not/ doesn´t leave
We leave	We do not/ don´t leave
You leave	You do not/ don´t leave
They leave	They do not/ don´t leave
POSITIVO (PRESENTE CONTINUO)	NEGATIVO
I am/ I´m leaving	Am I not/ aren´t I leaving?
You are/ you´re leaving	Are you not/ aren´t you leaving?
He/ she/it is/´s leaving	Is he/she/it not/isn´t he/she/it leaving?
We are/´re leaving	Are we not/ aren´t we leaving?
You are/ You´re leaving	Are you not/ aren´t you leaving?
They are/ ´re leaving	Are they not/ aren´t they leaving?

INTERROGATIVO (PRESENTE SIMPLE)
Do I/ not/ don´t I leave?
Do you not/ don´t you leave?
Does he/she/it not/ doesn´t he/she/it leave?
Do we/ not/ don´t we leave?
Do you not/ don´t you leave?
Do they not/ don´t they leave?
INTERROGATIVO (PRESENTE CONTINUO)
Am I/ not/ aren´t I leaving?
Are you/ not/ aren´t you leaving?
Is he/ she/ it not/isn´t he/ she/it leaving?
Are we/ not/ aren´t we leaving?
Are you/ not/ aren´t you leaving?
Are they/ not/ aren´t they leaving?

PRACTICE A: Find the Spanish meanings of the following verbs and conjugate them accordingly in English like the example above. (YouTube)

1. To come-

POSITIVO (PRESENTE SIMPLE)	NEGATIVO

POSITIVO (PRESENTE CONTINUO)	NEGATIVO

INTERROGATIVO (PRESENTE SIMPLE)

INTERROGATIVO (PRESENTE CONTINUO)

2. To say –

3.

POSITIVO (PRESENTE SIMPLE)	NEGATIVO

POSITIVO (PRESENTE CONTINUO)	NEGATIVO

INTERROGATIVO (PRESENTE SIMPLE)

INTERROGATIVO (PRESENTE CONTINUO)

3. To tell-

POSITIVO (PRESENTE SIMPLE)	NEGATIVO

POSITIVO (PRESENTE CONTINUO)	NEGATIVO

INTERROGATIVO (PRESENTE SIMPLE)

INTERROGATIVO (PRESENTE CONTINUO)

4. To do-

POSITIVO (PRESENTE SIMPLE)	NEGATIVO

POSITIVO (PRESENTE CONTINUO)	NEGATIVO

INTERROGATIVO (PRESENTE SIMPLE)

INTERROGATIVO (PRESENTE CONTINUO)

5. To make –

POSITIVO (PRESENTE SIMPLE)	NEGATIVO

POSITIVO (PRESENTE CONTINUO)	NEGATIVO

INTERROGATIVO (PRESENTE SIMPLE)

INTERROGATIVO (PRESENTE CONTINUO)

6. To hear-

POSITIVO (PRESENTE SIMPLE)	NEGATIVO

POSITIVO (PRESENTE CONTINUO)	NEGATIVO

INTERROGATIVO (PRESENTE SIMPLE)

INTERROGATIVO (PRESENTE CONTINUO)

7. To put-

POSITIVO (PRESENTE SIMPLE)	NEGATIVO

POSITIVO (PRESENTE CONTINUO)	NEGATIVO

INTERROGATIVO (PRESENTE SIMPLE)

INTERROGATIVO (PRESENTE CONTINUO)

8. To bring-

POSITIVO (PRESENTE SIMPLE)	NEGATIVO

POSITIVO (PRESENTE CONTINUO)	NEGATIVO

INTERROGATIVO (PRESENTE SIMPLE)

INTERROGATIVO (PRESENTE CONTINUO)

PRACTICE B: Conversation Practice. Translate these questions into English and answer them in English using one of the "go-go" verbs from above. (YouTube)

1. ¿Sales mucho?
2. ¿Cuántos hermanos tienes?
3. ¿Quién viene a tu casa los domingos?
4. ¿Qué oyes fuera de tu casa por la mañana?
5. ¿Qué dices a un inglés en su cumpleaños?
6. ¿Qué normalmente pones en tu mesita de noche?
7. ¿Qué normalmente haces para la comida los domingos?
8. ¿Tienes un perro?
9. ¿Qué dices cuando estás enfadado?
10. ¿Vienes a España a menudo?
11. ¿Oyes mucho inglés donde vives?
12. ¿Dónde pones las llaves en la casa?
13. ¿Cuándo haces paella?
14. ¿Qué traes contigo a clase de inglés?

27. TO LIKE- GUSTAR

En inglés el verbo que usamos para hablar de cosa que nos gustan es "to like".

No funciona como "gustar", es un verbo normal que conugamos como los otros en presente. No hay singular y plural, depende en la persona no en la casa /s que nos gustan.

For example: Me gust<u>a</u> el fútbol - I like football
              <u>Nos</u> gust<u>an</u> los animales- We like animals.

No usamos artículo menos cuando sea una cosa en particular-
Me gusta el perro- I like the dog (a particular dog)
Me gustan la casas- I like the houses (particular houses)
No solemos usarlo en continuo, pero de vez en cuando si.
P.e I am/I´m liking this! - Me gusta esto!

Cuando sea una acción que nos gusta, por ejemplo: bailar, nadar, trabajar etc, en iglés utilizamos el "ing" no el infinitivo.

   I like/ don´t like danc<u>ing</u>
   I like/ don´t like swimm<u>ing</u>
   I like/ don´t like work<u>ing</u>

POSITIVO (PRESENTE SIMPLE)	NEGATIVO
I like	I do not/ don´t like
You like	You do not/ don´t like
He/she/it likes	He/ she/it does not/ doesn´t like
We like	We do not/ don´t like
You like	You do not/ don´t like
They like	They do not/ don´t like
POSITIVO (PRESENTE CONTINUO)	NEGATIVO
I am/ I´m liking	I am not/ I´m not liking
You are/´re liking	You are not/´re not liking
He/ she/ it is/´s liking	He/she/it is not/isn´t liking
We are/´re liking	We are not/´re not liking
You are/´re liking	You are not/´re not liking
They are/´re liking	They are not/´re not liking

INTERROGATIVO (PRESENTE SIMPLE)
Do I/ not/ don´t I like?
Do you/ not/ don´t you like?
Does he/ she/ it not/ doesn´t he/ she/ it like?
Do we/ not/ don´t we like?
Do you/ not/ don´t you like?
Do they/ not/ don´t you like?
INTERROGATIVO (PRESENTE CONTINUO)
Am I/ not/ aren´t I liking?
Are you/ not/ aren´t you liking?
Is he/ she/ it/ not/ isn´t he/she/it liking?
Are we/ not/ aren´t we liking?
Are you/ not/ aren´t you liking?
Are they/ not/ aren´t they liking?

PRACTICE A: Translate the following into English. (YouTube)

1. Les gusta nadar.
2. ¿Te gusta el chocolate?
3. Nos gustan los coches rápidos.
4. No nos está gustando nada.
5. ¿Os gusta leer?
6. A él, le gusta nadar.
7. Me gusta cantar.
8. ¿A él, no le gusta estudiar?
9. No nos gusta hablar español.
10. Nos gusta salir los sábados.
11. A ella, e gusta salir con los amigos.
12. ¿Te gusta estudiar el inglés?
13. Les gustan la comida española.
14. Me gustan los gatos.
15. No me gustan los perros.
16. ¿No te gusta el fútbol?
17. No nos gusta viajar en avion.
18. Me gustan estos zapatos.
19. ¿Te estás gustando esta situación?
20. ¿No les gustas?
21. A él, no le gusta hablar español.
22. A ella, le gusta beber café.
23. ¿No nos gusta el vino?
24. ¿Os gusta nadar en el mar?
25. ¿Les están gustando estar en Londrés?

28. TO LIKE/ LOVE -GUSTAR/ ENCANTA

Practica A: Traduzca estos gustos y practica preguntando y contestandolos como el ejemplo. (YouTube)
1. ¿Te gusta nadar?- Do you like swimming?

- I hate swimming- Odio nadar
- I do not/ don´t like swimming at all- No me gusta nada nadar
- I like swimming- Me gusta nadar
- I quite like swimming- Me gusta bastante nadar
- I like swimming a lot- Me gusta mucho nadar
- I love swimming- Me encanta nadar

1. bailar
2. los animales
3. comer carne
4. beber vino
5. ir al cine
6. leer
7. trabajar
8. el chocolate
9. la pasta
10. la lluvia
11. inglaterra
12. pasear
13. estudiar inglés
14. ir a la playa
15. tomar el sol
16. cocinar
17. limpiar
18. cantar karaoke
19. jugar golf
20. hacer deporte
21. ver la tele
22. hablar por teléfono
23. salir con amigos
24. comer en restaurantes
25. la fruta
26. los mariscos

29. TO GO - IR

Con este verbo siempre usamos "to" ("a") porque normalmente vamos "a" algún sitio. Por ejemplo:

    Voy a la fiesta- I am going to the party.
    Vamos al supermercado- We are going to the supermarket.
    No vamos a la iglesia los domingos- We do not/ don´t go to the church on Sundays.

POSITIVO (PRESENTE SIMPLE)	NEGATIVO
I go	I do not/ don´t go
You go	You do not/ don´t go
He/ she/ it goes	He/ she/ it does not/ doesn´t go
We go	We do not/ don´t go
You go	You do not/ don´t go
They go	They do not/ don´t go
POSITIVO (PRESENTE CONTINUO)	NEGATIVO
I am/ I´m going	I am not/ I´m not going
You are/ you´re going	You are not/ you´re not going
He/ she/it is/ ´s going	He/ she/ it is not/ isn´t going
We are/ we´re going	We are not/ we´re not going
You are/ you´re going	You are not/ you´re not going
They are/ they´re going	They are not/ they´re not going

INTERROGATIVO (PRESENTE SIMPLE)
Do I/ not/ don´t I go?
Do you/ not/ don´t you go?
Does he/ she/it/ not/ doesn´t he/she/it go?
Do we/ not/ don´t we go?
Do you/ not/ don´t you go?
Do they/ not/ don´t they go?
INTERROGATIVO (PRESENTE CONTINUO)
Am I/ not/ aren´t I going?
Are you/ not/ aren´t you going ?
Is he/ she/it /not/ isn´t he/she/it going?
Are we/ not/ aren´t we going?
Are you/ not/ aren´t you going?
Are they/ not/ aren´t they going?

PRACTICE A: Translate the following into English. (YouTube)

1. ¿Adónde vas?
2. Van a la playa todas las semanas.
3. Vamos al bar cada domingo.
4. ¿Adónde vas los sábados?
5. Va al trabajo en el autobús.
6. Voy al hospital cada martes por la mañana.
7. Cuando necesito verduras, voy al mercadillo.
8. Mi hermano siempre va al futból.
9. Para conseguir un permiso, tenéis que ir al Ayuntamiento.
10. ¿Cuándo van al cine?
11. Voy a España cada año.
12. Vamos a su casa los lunes.
13. Van a su casa los martes.
14. ¿Vas mucho a las tiendas?
15. ¿Por qué no vas a su casa?

30. AUNT KATHY / TIA KATHY.

PRACTICE A: IDENTIFY THE 46 VERBS IN THIS TEXT AND USE THEM TO COMPLETE THE VERB IDENTIFICATION TABLE AS PER THE EXAMPLE.

Kathy Brown es mi tia, la hermana de mi madre. Vive en el sur de Inglaterra. Vive en un apartamento pequeño, limpio y ordenado en el centro de la ciudad de Reading. Vive sola pero tiene una gata pequeño y blanco. El nombre de la gata es "Luna".

Kathy es alta, morena, y tiene ojos grises. Es muy guapa y tiene treinta y cinco años. No está casada pero tiene un novio, Lewis. Aunt Kathy es abogada y tiene una oficina grande cerca de su casa.

Termina el trabajo a las siete de la tarde y cuando llega a casa está muy cansada. En su apartamento hay dos dormitorios, un cuarto de baño, un salón, y un despacho.

Sube las escaleras porque, a ella, no le gustan los ascensores y quiere hacer más ejercicio. Cuando llega al tercer piso saca su llave, abre la puerta y entra. Luna siempre viene para decir hola. Hace mucho ruido para una gata.

Kathy entra en el despacho y enciende el ordenador. Después entra en la cocina donde hace un café. Vuelve al despacho y lee sus correos elétronicos. Se sienta y empieza leerlos.

Entonces apaga el ordenador y seva a la cocina donde prepara la cena, después enciende la television en el salón. Su novio Lewis a menudo la llama por teléfono. Charlan durante un rato corto, y entonces Kathy lavalos platos y decide acostarse.

VERB IN CONTEXT	INFINITIVE	SPANISH	PERSON
1.			
2.			
3.			
4.			
5.			
6.			
7.			
8.			

9.			
10.			
11.			
12.			
13.			
14.			
15.			
16.			
17.			
18.			
19.			
20.			
21.			
22.			
23.			
24.			
25.			
26.			
27.			
28.			
29.			
30.			
31.			
32.			
33.			
34.			
35.			
36.			
37.			
38.			
39.			
40.			
41.			
42.			
43.			
44.			
45.			
46.			

PRACTICE B: Translate the text into English.

PRACTICE C: Translate the questions into English and answer in English.

1. ¿Dónde vive Kathy Brown?
2. ¿Cómo es su apartamento y dónde está?
3. ¿Con quién vive?
4. ¿Cuántos años tiene?
5. ¿Está casada?
6. ¿Qué hace y dónde trabaja?
7. ¿A qué hora termina el trabajo?
8. ¿Cómo está cuando llega a casa?
9. ¿Qué hay en su apartamento?
10. ¿Por qué sube las escaleras?
11. ¿Qué hace cuando llega al tercer piso?
12. ¿Quién viene para decir "hola"?
13. ¿Qué hace en la oficina?
14. ¿Qué hace en la cocina?
15. ¿Dónde lee sus correos electrónicos?
16. ¿Qué hace después de contestarlos?
17. ¿Quién la llama a menudo por teléfono?
18. ¿Qué hace Kathy después de lavar los platos?

31. POSTSCRIPT

Espero que hayas disfrutado de este libro y tu inglés haya mejorado.
Repasa los ejercicios con mucha frecuencia y practica hablar y escuchar lo más posible. La repetición y la practica es fudemental para la fluidez y confianza. Pero acuérdate: no te esperas demasiado. Te equivocarás mucho antes de acertarse!!

Practica lo más posible. Escucha la radio inglesa, ve la tele inglesa. Véte al cine inglés y cambia tu Netflix al idioma inglés. Cuando tengas confianza en todo de este Nivel 1, sabrás comunicar efectivamente en inglés y estarás preparad@ a empezar con Nivel 2.

Happy practicing!!

Vicki

¿DUDAS? ¿PREGUNTAS? ¿COMENTARIOS?

info@elprincipecentre.com

32. CLAVE "TOP TIPS"/ KEY TO "TOP TIPS"   PÁGINA

1. VERBOS AUXILIARES   7
2. QUESTION TAG.   8
3. "CLOTH"/ "CLOTHES"   14
4. PALABRAS INTERROGATIVAS/ QUESTION WORDS   20
5. LA DIFERENCIA ENTRE PRESENTE SIMPLE Y CONTINUO   24
6. LA DIFERENCIA ENTRE "SPEAK" Y "TALK".   25
7. VERBO "TO GO"- IR   32
8. GENITIVO SAJÓN   40
9. VERBO "TO HAVE" / TOMAR   51
10. LAS PARTES DEL CUERPO   69
11. PRONOMBRES POSESIVOS   109

33. ANSWERS/ RESPUESTAS

1. ALPHABET AND PRONUNCIATION

PRACTICE B:

A- manzana
B- balón/pelota
C- gato/a
D- perro/a
E- huevo
F- pez/pescado
G- cabra
H- sombrero
I- iglú
J- gelatina
K- cometa
L- hoja
M- luna
N- nido
O- naranja
P- pingüino/a
Q- reina
R- anillo
S- sol
T- árbol
U- paraguas
V- florero
W- ballena
X- radiografia
Y- amarillo
Z- cebra

2. MASCULINE AND FEMININE

PRACTICE A: (YouTube)

1. The office.
2. A doctor.
3. The car.
4. A skirt.
5. The star.
6. An orange.
7. The supermarket.
8. A computer.
9. The airport.
10. The teacher.
11. An elephant.
12. The magazine.
13. A dog.
14. The chair.

PRACTICE B: (YouTube)

1. The flowers.
2. Some potatoes.
3. The drinks.
4. Some buildings.
5. The banks.
6. Some shops.
7. The tables.
8. Some newspapers.
9. The telephones.
10. Some cupboards/ wardrobes.
11. The kitchens.
12. Some gardens.
13. The women.
14. Some boys.

4. PRACTICA LOS NÚMEROS

PRACTICE A: (YouTube)

1. One hundred and twenty-one.
2. Five hundred and sixty-seven.
3. Fifty-four.
4. One thousand, four hundred and fifty-seven.
5. Nine hundred and ninety-nine.
6. Six hundred and thirty-two.
7. Thirty-two.
8. Seven hundred and sixty-eight.
9. Two thousand, five hundred and thirty.
10. Five thousand, three hundred and twenty-four.
11. Seven hundred and twenty-four.
12. Seventeen.
13. Eight hundred and fifty-two.
14. Fifteen.
15. Sixty-one.
16. Three hundred and thirty-three.
17. One thousand and twenty-three.
18. One hundred and fifty-five.
19. Five hundred and ninety-two.
20. Four hundred and thirty-one.
21. Seventy-seven.
22. Eight hundred and eighty-eight.
23. Nine hundred and twnty-three.
24. Sixty-seven.
25. Two hundred and seventy-four.
26. Ninety-two.
27. Five thousand, two hundred and thirty two.
28. Twenty-four.
29. Eighty-seven.
30. One hundred and sixty-five.

5. ROPA Y NÚMEROS

PRACTICE A:

1. How much do the gloves cost? – The gloves cost twenty-five pounds.
2. How much does the shirt cost? The shirt costs thirty-one pounds and ninety-nine pence.
3. How much does the scarf cost? The scarf costs nine pounds and ninety-nine pence

4. How much do the trousers cost? The trousers cost fifteen pounds and forty-four pence.
5. How much do the shoes cost? The shoes cost eighteen pounds and seventy pence.
6. How much do the socks cost? The socks cost nine pounds and ninety-nine pence.
7. How much does the jumper cost? The jumper costs thirty-three pounds and sixty pence.
8. How much does the skirt cost? The skirt costs forty-seven pounds and twenty pence.
9. How much does the jacket cost? The jacket costs forty-five pounds and twenty pence.
10. How much does the t-shirt cost? The t-shirt costs thirty-three pounds and sixty-two pence.
11. How much does the dress cost? The dress costs ninety pounds.
12. How much does the hat cost? The hat costs eighteen pounds and seventy-one pence.

6. WHAT TIME IS IT? - ¿QUÉ HORA ES?

PRACTICE A:

1. It is/it´s half- past eleven/ eleven thirty.
2. It is/it´s quarter to four/ three fourty-five.
3. It is/it´s ten past one.
4. It is/it´s twenty to one/ twelve forty.
5. It is/it´s two o´clock.
6. It is/it´s twenty-five past eight.
7. It is/it´s twenty past nine.
8. It is/it´s twenty-five past one.
9. It is/it´s half- past ten/ ten thirty.
10. It is/it´s quarter to nine/ eight forty-five.

PRACTICANDO LA HORA/ PRACTICING THE TIME

PRACTICE B:

1. What time does the train (tren) leave? The train leaves at ten fifteen/ quarter past ten.
   What time does the train arrive? The train arrives at eight o´clock.

ROMPER LA BARRERA DEL IDIOMA INGLÉS NIVEL 1
WWW.ELPRINCIPECENTRE.COM
info@elprincipecentre.com

2. What time does the bus (aútobus) leave? The bus leaves at ten past eleven.
   What time does the bus arrive? The bus arrives at half past five/ five-thirty.
3. What time does the aeroplane (avión) leave? The aeroplane leaves at ten-twenty/ twenty past ten.
   What time does the aeroplane arrive? The aeroplane arrives at three ten/ ten past three.
4. What time does the postman (cartero) leave? The postman leaves at five past ten/ ten oh five.
   What time does the postman arrive? The postman arrives at three ten/ ten past three.
5. What time does the doctor (medico) leave? The doctor leaves at eight forty-five/ quarter to eight.
   What time does the doctor arrive? The doctor arrives at nine forty-five/ quarter to ten.
6. What time does the nurse (enfermera) leave? The nurse leaves at twelve thirty-five/ twenty-five to one.
   What time does the nurse arrive? The nurse arrives at one fifteen/ quarter past one.
7. What time does the secretary (secretaria) leave? The secretary leaves at four forty-five/ quarter to five.
   What time does the secretary arrive? The secretary arrives at half-past two/two-thirty.
8. What time does the woman (la señora) leave? The woman leaves at five-fifty/ ten to six.
   What time does the woman arrive? The woman arrives at six-forty/ twenty to seven.
9. What time does the teacher (el professor) leave? The teacher leaves at three twenty-five/ twenty-five past three.
   What time does the teacher arrive? The teacher arrives at eleven twenty-five/ twenty-five past eleven.
10. What time does Susan leave? Susan leaves at one twenty/ twenty past one.
    What time does Susan arrive? Susan arrives at five past six/ six oh five.

PRACTICE C:

1. What time does the match (partido) start? The match starts at ten fifteen/ quarter past ten.

What time does the match finish? The match finishes at twelve fifteen/ quarter past twelve.

2. What time does the programme (el programa) start? The programme starts at four fifteen.

What time does the programme finish? The programme finishes at five thirty/ half past five.

3. What time does the show (el espectáculo) start? The show starts at ten twenty/ twenty past ten.

What time does the show finish? The show finishes at ten past three.

4. What time does the exhibition (la feria) start? The exhibition starts at nine twenty/ twenty past nine.

What time does the exhibition finish? The exhibition finishes at seven forty/ twenty to eight.

5. What time does the singer (el cantante) start? The singer starts at eight forty-five /quarter to nine.

What time does the singer finish? The singer finishes at nine forty-five / quarter to ten.

6. What time does the meal (la comida) start? The meal starts at one thirty/ half-past one.

What time does the meal finish? The meal finishes at three fifty/ ten to four.

7. What time does the party (la fiesta) start? The party starts at four forty-five/ quarter to five.

What time does the party finish? The party finishes at two thirty/ half-past two.

8. What time does the dinner (la cena) start? The dinner starts at ten past ten.

What time does the dinner finish? The dinner finishes at one fifteen/ quarter past one.

9. What time does the class (la clase) start? The class starts at three twenty-five/ twenty-five past three.

What time does the class finish? The class finishes at eleven oh five/ five past eleven.

10. What time does the dance (el baile) start? The dance starts at eleven thirty/ half-past eleven.

What time does the dance finish? The dance finishes at four o´clock.

7. EL VERBO "TO BE" - "SER" O "ESTAR"

PRACTICE A: RESPUESTA LIBRE

PRACTICE B: (YOUTUBE)

1. We are/we´re English.
2. The table is square.
3. I am/I´m with my friend.
4. I am not/I´m not with my friend.
5. Are you a doctor?
6. Are you teachers?
7. We are tired.
8. You are happy.
9. She is not/isn´t very tall.
10. They are not/they´re not/they aren´t from Spain.
11. I am/I´m Juan.
12. Pedro and Carmen are in Spain.
13. I am/I´m sad because you are not/aren´t/ you´re not here.
14. Why are you not/aren´t you happy?
15. He is/he´s a waiter.
16. I am/I´m from the United States.
17. You are not/aren´t my friends.
18. He is/ he´s handsome.
19. Is he married or single?
20. She is/ she´s in class and he is/ he´s in the garden.
21. We are/we´re angry.
22. The sky is not/isn´t grey.
23. Jane is divorced.
24. The coffee is cold.
25. She is not/ isn´t very interesting.
26. They are/they´re French from Paris.
27. You are/you´re teachers.
28. Today is not/isn´t Tuesday.
29. My socks are white.
30. Who are you?
31. Who are you?
32. Jennifer Aniston is/´s an actress.

8. EL VERBO "TO BE" EN CONTEXTO - THE VERB "TO BE" IN CONTEXT

PRACTICE B: Verbos

1. I´m
2. I´m
3. I´m
4. Are you
5. I´m
6. Are they
7. They´re
8. is
9. is
10. is
11. ´s
12. is
13. ´s
14. He is
15. Is he
16. He´s

TRANSLATION

Pedro: Hola! Soy Pedro.
Ana: Yo soy Ana.
Pedro: Encantado. Soy español, de Madrid. ¿Y tú Ana? ¿De dónde eres?
Ana: Soy rusa de Moscú.
Pedro: ¿Son ellos también rusos?
Ana: No, no son rusos..Paulo es italiano, de Roma. Claudia es francesa, de Paris. Paco es sudamericano, de Columbia. ¿Quién es el profesor de inglés?
Pedro: John Jones es el profesor.
Ana: ¿Cómo es John Jones?
Pedro: Es alto, moreno y muy simpático.
Ana: ¿Es inglés o americano?
Pedro: Es inglés de Londrés.

PRACTICE C: (Audio 10)

1. Where is Pedro from? Pedro is Spanish, from Madrid.
2. Where is Ana from? Ana is Russian, from Moscow
3. Is Paulo Italian? Yes, Paulo is Italian, from Rome.
4. Is Claudia German? No, Claudia is not/ isn´t German. She is/she´s French from Paris.
5. Where is/´s Paco from? Paco is South American, from Columbia
6. Who is/´s the teacher? John Jones is the teacher.

7. What is/´s John Jones? John Jones is the teacher.
8. What is/´s John Jones like? He is/he´s tall, dark, and very nice.
9. Where is/´s John Jones from?
10. Where are you from? Free answer

PRACTICE D: (YOUTUBE)

JUAN: Hello, I am/I´m Juan. Who are you?
CARMEN: I am/I´m Carmen. Are you an English student?
JUAN: No, I´m not an English student, I am/ I´m a German student. And you?
CARMEN: I am/ I´m a German student too.
JUAN: Where are you from?
CARMEN: I am/ I´m Spanish from Alicante. And you?.
JUAN: I am/ I´m Spanish too, from Seville.
CARMEN: Who is/ ´s the German teacher?
JUAN: Señora Schmidt.
CARMEN: What is/ ´s she like and where is/ ´s she from?
JUAN: She is/ ´s short, blonde and very nice. She is/ ´s from Munich.

PRACTICE E: (YOUTUBE)

1. Is Juan an English student? No, he is not/ isn´t an English student, he is/ he´s a German student.
2. Is Carmen an English student? No, she is not/ isn´t an English student. She is/ ´s a German student too.
3. Where is Carmen from? Carmen is Spanish, from Alicante
4. Where is Juan from? Juan is Spanish too, from Seville.
5. Who is/ ´s the German teacher? Mrs Schmidt is the German teacher.
6. What is/ ´s Mrs Scmidt like? She is/ she´s short, blonde and very nice.
7. Who is/ ´s your English teacher? Free answer
8. What is/ ´s he or she like? Free answer
9. Where are/ where´re you from? Free answer
10. What are/ ´re you like? Free answer

9. THE VERB "TO BE" IN CONTEXT 2 - EN LA CLASE

PRACTICE B: Verbos

1. Are you
2. I am
12. It is
13. It is

ROMPER LA BARRERA DEL IDIOMA INGLÉS NIVEL 1
WWW.ELPRINCIPECENTRE.COM
info@elprincipecentre.com

3. I´m
4. is
5. she´s
6. she´s
7. is she
8. is
9. it´s
10. are you
11. I´m
14. is
15. I´m
16. I´m not
17. is
18. It´s
19. Are you
20. I am

PRACTICE C:

Paul : Buenos días Susan. ¿Cómo estás?
Susan: Estoy muy bien, gracias. Y tú?
Paul: Estoy muy bien también. ¿Dónde está tu hermana Carol?
Susan: No está en clase hoy, Está en casa.
Paul: ¿Por qué? ¿Está enferma?
Susan: Si, está resfriada.
Paul: ¿Dónde está la casa?
Susan: Está en Calle de Sherwood, número 18, a la izquierda de la calle.
Paul: Gracias.
(En la casa de Carol)
Paul: Hola Carol. ¿Cómo estás?
Carol: Estoy resfriada. Pero hoy estoy un poco mejor.
Paul: Me gusta to casa, es muy bonita.
Carol: Si, pero hoy está muy desordenada. ¿Está abierta la puerta? Tengo frio, no estoy cómoda.
Paul: Si, la puerta está abierta. Ahora está cerrada. ¿Estás cómoda ahora?
Carol: Si, ahora estoy bien.

PRACTICE D: (YouTube)

1. How is Susan? Susan is/´s fine
2. Where is her sister Carol? She is/ she´s at home.
3. Is she ill? Yes, she has a cold.
4. Where is the house? The house is on Sherwood Street, number 18, on the left of the street.
5. How is/ How´s Carol today? Today she is/ she´s a little better.
6. What is/ what´s the house like? The house is very pretty.
7. What is it/ what´s it like today? Today it is/ it´s very untidy.

8. Is Carol comfortable? No, she is not/ she isnt comfortable/ she is cold/she´s cold.

9. Why is she/ why´s she cold? The door is/´s open.

10. Is she comfortable now? Yes, now she is/´s fine.

11. How are you today? Free answer.

12. Are you comfortable? Free answer.

10. CONVERSATION PRACTICE WITH THE VERB "TO BE". FREE ANSWERS.

PRACTICE A:

1. Where are you from?
2. Where is your house?
3. What is your house like?
4. When is Christmas?
5. Where is Buckingham Palace?
6. Why is English important?
7. What is Spain like?
8. Who is your best friend?
9. Where is your car?
10. When is your birthday?
11. Are you tired?
12. Are you happy?
13. What colour is your car?
14. Which/what day is/´s it?
15. Who are/´re you with?
16. Which is better, the country or the beach?
17. Are you at home?
18. Who is/´s your favorite actor?
19. Which/what is/´s your favorite food?
20. What is important in your life?

11. DESCRIBING PEOPLE

PRACTICA B:

1. Él es español y tiene más o menos cuarenta y cinco años. Es alto y moreno con ojos castaños/ marrones. Es muy guapo con peolo moreno y rizado. Es cantante. Su padre

también es un cantante español muy famoso. Está casado con una jugadora de tenis muy famosa y tienen trs niños. Dos de sus niños son gemelos. ¿Quien es?
ENRIQUE IGLESIAS

2. Es Columbiana. Es muy guapa con pelo largo, rubio y ondulado. Tiene más o menos cuarenta y cinco años. No está casada pero tiene dos hijos. Su pareja actual es un futbolista español y tiene diez años menos que ella. Una de sus canciones mas famosas es En inglés y habla de una parte del cuerpo que no mienta. Ws famosa por todo el mundo. ¿Quién es?
SHAKIRA.

3. Son ingleses. Están casados y tienen cuatro hijos, tres chicos y una chica. Él es futbolista jubilado y ella es mujer de negocios, antes cantante en un grupo británico de chicas muy famoso. Él es rubio, Delgado, muy guapo y normalmente tiene barba y bigote cortos. Tiene ojos azules. Ella es muy delgada y tiene pelo moreno. Ella tiene ojos castaños. Los dos tienen más o menos cuarenta y seis años. ¿Quiénes son?
LOS BECKHAM

12. THERE IS / THERE ARE- HAY (FREE ANSWERS)

1. How many bedrooms are there in your house?
2. Is there a television in your bedroom?
3. Are there any flowers in your garden?
4. Are there any pictures in your living room?
5. Are there any pets in your house?
6. How many trees are there in your garden?
7. Are there any good restaurants near your house?
8. Are there many books in your house?
9. Is there a car in fromt of your house?
10. What is there on your bedside table?

13. HAY/ SER/ ESTAR- THERE IS/ THERE ARE/ "TO BE"

1. HAY

Una mesa/ uns mesas   una revista/ unas revistas
Una silla/ unas sillas   un periódico/unos periódicos
Una ventana/ unas ventanas   una televisión/unas televisiones
Un cuadro/ unos cuadros   un libro/ unos libros

Una lámpara/ unas lámparas una luz/ unas luces
Una mesita de café/ unas mesitas de café un sofá/ unos sofas
Una alfombra/ unas alfombras una estantería/ unas estanterías

2. ES/SON- ESTÁ/ESTÁN

PRACTICE A:

A la izquierda/ derecha	En el centro de
Sobre	En el rincón
En	Alrededor de
Encima de	En la pared
En/ dentro	Debajo de
Delante de	Entre
Detrás de	Cerca
Al lado de	Bonito/a/s
Alto/a/s	Cuadrado/a/s
Bajo/a/s	Redondo/a/s
Largo/a/s	Grande/s
Rectángulo/a/s	Pequeño/a/s
Estrecho/a/s	Ancho/a/s

PRACTICE C: FREE ANSWER

14. LA CASA DE JOHN- JOHN´S HOUSE

PRACTICE B:

1. Is
2. He´s
3. He´s
4. He is
5. He´s
6. Is he
7. He is
8. There are
9. John is
10. What is
11. It is

12. There is
13. There is
14. A dog is
15. John´s mother is
16. The armchair is
17. Pedro is
18. What is there
19. There is
20. There is
21. There is
22. There is
23. The television is

PRACTICE C:

John Jones es inglés. Es de Manchester. Es camarero. Es alto, rubio, y tiene ojos azules y gafas. Es muy simpático. ¿Dónde está hoy? Hoy está en casa. En la casa hay dos dormitorios, un cuarto de baño, una cocina y un salón. John está en el salón.

¿Cómo es el salón? Es muy grande- En el salón hay una mesa, un sofá, un sillón, unas sillas y una televisión. En el suelo hay una alfombra. Un perro está sentado en la alfombra debajo de una silla. La madre de John está sentada en un sillón. El sillón es muy cómodo. Pedro está sentado el el sofá.

¿Qué hay en la mesa? En la mesa hay una taza in en la taza hay café. Hay también una revista y unos libros. En la pared hay un espejo y unos cuadros. La televisión está debajo del espejo.

PRACTICE D:

1. Where is John from? John is/ ´s from Manchester.
2. What is John? John is/ ´s a waiter.
3. What is John like? John is/ ´s tall, blonde and has grey eyes.
4. Where is he today? Today he is/´s at home.
5. How many bedrooms are there in his house? There are two bedrooms in his house.
6. What is the living room like? It is very big.
7. What is there on the floor? There is/ ´s a rug on the floor.
8. Where is/ ´s the dog? The dog is sitting on the rug.
9. Where is John´s mother? John´s mother is sitting in an armchair.

10. What is there on the table? On the table there is a cup and in the cup there is coffee. Also there is a magazine and some books.
11. Where are the pictures? The pictures are on the wall.
12. Where is the television? The television is under the mirror.

15. REGULAR VERBS - 1ST CONJUGATION – 'AR' VERBS

PRACTICE A:

2. To dance - bailar

POSITIVO (PRESENTE SIMPLE)	NEGATIVO
I dance	I do not/don´t dance
You dance	You do not/don´t dance
He/ she/ it dances	He/ she/ it does not/ doesn´t dance
We dance	We do not/don´t dance
You dance	You do not/ don´t dance
They dance	They do not/ don´t dance
POSITIVO (CONTINUO)	**NEGATIVO**
I am/ I´m dancing	I am/ I´m not dancing
You are/ you´re dancing	You are/ you´re/not/ aren´t dancing
He/she/it is/ ´s dancing	He/she/it is not/isn´t dancing
We are/we´re dancing	We are not/ aren´t dancing
You are/you´re dancing	You are/ you´re not/ aren´t dancing
They are/ they´re dancing	They are /they´re not/aren´t dancing

INTERROGATIVO (PRESENTE SIMPLE)
Do I/ do I not/ don´t I dance?
Do you/ do you not/ don´t you dance?
Does he/she/it not/doesn´t he/she/it dance?
Do we not/ don´t we dance?
Do you/ do you not/ don´t you dance?
Do they not/ don´t they dance?
INTERROGATIVO (PRESENTE CONTINUO)
Am I not/ Aren´t I dancing?
Are you/ are you not/ aren´t you dancing?
Is he/she/it/ isn´t he she or it dancing?
Are we/ are we not/ aren´t we dancing?
Are you/ are you not/ aren´t you dancing?
Are they/ are they not/ aren´t they dancing?

3. To look for - buscar

POSITIVO (PRESENTE SIMPLE)	NEGATIVO
I look for	I do not/ don´t look for
You look for	You do not/ don´t look for
He/ she/it looks for	He/she/it does not/ doesn´t look for
We look for	We do not/don´t look for
You look for	You do not/ don´t look for
They look for	We do not/ don´t look for
POSITIVO (PRESENTE CONTINUO)	NEGATIVO
I am/ I´m looking for	I am/ I´m not/looking for
You are/ you´re looking for	You are/ you´re not/ aren´t looking for
He/ she/it is/ ´s looking for	He/ she/ it is not/ isn´t looking for
We are/ we´re looking for	We are/we´re not/ aren´t looking for
You are/ you´re looking for	You are/ you´re not/ aren´t looking for
They are/ ´re looking for	They are/ they´re not/ aren´t looking for

INTERROGATIVO (PRESENTE SIMPLE)
Do I/ do I not/ don´t I look for?
Do you/ do you not/ don´t you look for?
Does he/she/it not/doesn´t he/she/it look for?
Do we not/ don´t we look for?
Do you/ do you not/ don´t you look for?
Do they not/ don´t they look for?
INTERROGATIVO (PRESENTE CONTINUO)
Am I /not/ aren´t I looking for?
Are you not/ aren´t you looking for?
Is he/she/it/ isn´t he she or it looking for?
Are we/ are we not/ aren´t we looking for?
Are you not/ aren´t you looking for?
Are they/ are they not/ aren´t they looking for?

4. To sing - cantar

POSITIVO (PRESENTE SIMPLE)	NEGATIVO
I sing	I do not/don´t sing
You sing	You do not/don´t sing
He/ she/it sings	He/she/it doesn´t sing
We sing	We do not/don´t sing
You sing	You do not/don´t sing
They sing	We do not/don´t sing
POSITIVO (PRESENTE CONTINUO)	NEGATIVO
I am/ I´m singing	I am not/ I´m not singing
You are/ you´re singing	You are/ you´re not/ aren´t singing
He/ she/ it is/ ´s singing	He/ she/ it is not/isn´t singing
We are/we´re singing	We are not/ we´re not/aren´t singing
You are/ you´re singing	You are/ you´re not/ aren´t singing
They are/ they´re singing	They are/ they´re not/ aren´t singing

INTERROGATIVE (PRESENTE SIMPLE)
Do I/ do I not/ don´t I sing?
Do you not/ don´t you sing?
Does he/ she/ it not/ doesn´t he/ she/ it sing?
Do we not/ don´t we sing?
Do you not/ don´t you sing?
Do they not/ don´t they sing?
INTERROGATIVE (PRESENTE CONTINUO)
Am I /not/ aren´t I singing?
Are you not/ aren´t you singing?
Is he/she/it/ isn´t he she or it singing?
Are we/ are we not/ aren´t we singing?
Are you not/ aren´t you singing?
Are they/ are they not/ aren´t they singing?

5. To study- estudiar

POSITIVO (PRESENTE SIMPLE)	NEGATIVO
I study	I do not/ don´t study
You study	You do not/ don´t study
He/she/it studies	He/she/it does not/ doesn´t study
We study	We do not/ don´t study
You study	You do not/ don´t study
They study	They do not/ don´t study
POSITIVO (PRESENTE CONTINUO)	NEGATIVO
I am/ I´m studying	I am not/ I´m not studying
You are/ you´re studying	You are/ you´re not/ aren´t studying
He/ she / it is/ ´s studying	He/ she/ it is/ ´s not/isn´t studying
We are/ we´re studying	We are not/ ´re/ not/aren´t studying
You are/ you´re studying	You are/ you´re not/ aren´t studying
They are/ they´re studying	They are/ ´re not/aren´t studying

INTERROGATIVE (PRESENTE SIMPLE)
Do I/ do I not/ don´t I study?
Do you/ do you not/ don´t you study?
Does he/ she/ it/ not/ doesn´t he/ she/ it study?
Do we/ do we not/ don´t we study?
Do you/ do you not/ don´t you study?
Do they/ do they not/ don´t they study?
INTERROGATIVE (PRESENTE CONTINUO)
Am I /not/ aren´t I studying?
Are you not/ aren´t you studying?
Is he/she/it/ isn´t he she or it studying?
Are we not/ aren´t we studying?
Are you not/ aren´t you studying?
Are they not/ aren´t they studying?

6. To buy - comprar

POSITIVO (PRESENTE SIMPLE)	NEGATIVO
I buy	I do not/ don´t buy
You buy	You do not/ don´t buy
He/ she/it buys	He/ she it does not/ doesn´t buy
We buy	We do not/ don´t buy
You buy	You do not/ don´t buy
They buy	They do not/ don´t buy
POSITIVO (PRESENTE CONTINUO)	NEGATIVO
I am/ I´m buying	I am not/ ´m not buying
You are/ you´re buying	You are not/ ´re not/ aren´t buying
He/ she/ it is/ ´s buying	He/ she/ it is/ ´s not/isn´t buying
We are/ we´re buying	We are not/ ´re/ not/aren´t buying
You are/ you´re buying	You are not/ ´re not/ aren´t buying
They are/ they´re buying	They are not/ ´re/ not/aren´t buying

INTERROGATIVE (PRESENTE SIMPLE)
Do I/ do I not/ don´t I buy?
Do you/ do you not/ don´t you buy?
Does he/ she/ it/ not/ doesn´t he/ she/ it buy?
Do we/ do we not/ don´t we buy?
Do you/ do you not/ don´t you buy?
Do they/ do they not/ don´t they buy?
INTERROGATIVE (PRESENTE CONTINUO)
Am I /not/ aren´t I buying?
Are you not/ aren´t you buying?
Is he/she/it/ isn´t he she or it buying?
Are we/ not/ aren't we buying?
Are you not/ aren´t you buying?
Are they not/ aren´t they buying?

7. To listen- escuchar

POSITIVO (PRESENTE SIMPLE)	NEGATIVO
I listen	I do not/ don´t listen
You listen	You do not/ don´t listen
He/ she/ it listens	He/she/it does not/ doesn´t listen
We listen	We do not/ don´t listen
You listen	You do not/ don´t listen
We listen	They do not/ don´t listen
POSITIVO (PRESENTE CONTINUO)	NEGATIVO
I am/ I´m listening	I am not/ ´m not listening
You are/ you´re listening	You are not/ ´re not/ aren´t listening
He/she/it is/´s listening	He/ she/ it is/ ´s not/isn´t listening
We are/ we´re listening	We are not/ ´re/ not/aren´t listening
You are/ you´re listening	You are not/ ´re not/ aren´t listening
They are/ they´re listening	They are not/ ´re/ not/aren´t listening

INTERROGATIVO (PRESENTE SIMPLE)
Do I/ do I not/ don´t I listen?
Do you/ do you not/ don´t you listen?
Does he/ she/ it/ not/ doesn´t he/ she/ it listen?
Do we/ do we not/ don´t we listen?
Do you/ do you not/ don´t you listen?
Do they/ do they not/ don´t they listen?
INTERROGATIVO (PRESENTE CONTINUO)
Am I /not/ aren´t I listening?
Are you not/ aren´t you listening?
Is he/she/it/ isn´t he she or it listening?
Are we/ not/ aren't we listening?
Are you not/ aren´t you listening?
Are they/ not/ aren't they buying?

8. To wait for- esperar

POSITIVO (PRESENTE SIMPLE)	NEGATIVO
I wait for	I do not/ don´t wait for
You wait for	You do not/ don´t wait for
He/ she/ it waits for	He/ she/it does not/ doesn´t wait for
We wait for	We do not/ don´t wait for
You wait for	You do not/ don´t wait for
They wait for	They do not/ don´t wait for
POSITIVO (PRESENTE CONTINUO)	NEGATIVO
I am/ I´m waiting for	I am not/ ´m not waiting for
You are/ you´re waiting for	You are not/ ´re not/ aren´t waiting for
He/ she/ it is /´s waiting for	He/she/it is not/ isn´t waiting for
We are/ we´re waiting for	We are not/ ´re/ not/aren´t waiting for
You are/ you´re waiting for	You are not/ ´re not/ aren´t waiting for
They are/ they´re waiting for	They are/´re not/ aren´t waiting for

INTERROGATIVE (PRESENTE SIMPLE)
Do I/ do I not/ don´t I wait for?
Do you/ do you not/ don´t you wait for?
Does he/ she/ it/ not/ doesn´t he/ she/ it wait for?
Do we/ do we not/ don´t we wait for?
Do you/ do you not/ don´t you wait for?
Do you/ do you not/ don´t you wait for?
INTERROGATIVE (PRESENTE CONTINUO)
Am I not/ aren´t I waiting for?
Are you not/ aren´t you waiting for?
Is he/she/it/ isn´t he she or it waiting for?
Are we not/ aren´t we waiting for?
Are you not/ aren´t you waiting for?
Are they not/ aren´t they waiting for?

9. To arrive- llegar

POSITIVO (PRESENTE SIMPLE)	NEGATIVO
I arrive	I do not/ don´t arrive
You arrive	You do not/ don´t arrive
He/ she/ it arrives	He/ she/ it does not/ doesn´t arrive
We arrive	We do not/ don´t arrive
You rrive	You do not/ don´t arrive
They arrive	They do not/ don´t arrive
POSITIVO (PRESENTE CONTINUO)	NEGATIVO
I am/ I´m arriving	I am / I´m not arriving
You are/ you´re arriving	You are not/ ´re not/ aren´t arriving
He/ she/ it is/´s arriving	He/she/it is not/ isn´t arriving
We are/ we´re arriving	We are not/ ´re not/ aren´t arriving
You are/ you´re arriving	You are not/ ´re not/ aren´t arriving
They are/ they´re arriving	They are not/ ´re not/ aren´t arriving

INTERROGATIVO (PRESENTE SIMPLE)
Do I/ do I not/ don´t I arrive?
Do you/ do you not/ don´t you arrive?
Does he/ she/ it not/ doesn´t he/she/ it arrive?
Do we/ do we not/ don´t we arrive?
Do you/ do you not/ don´t you arrive?
Do they/ do they not/ don´t they arrive
INTERROGATIVO (PRESENTE CONTINUO)
Am I not/ aren´t I arriving?
Are you not/ aren´t you arriving?
Is he/she/it/ isn´t he she or it arriving?
Are we not/ aren´t we arriving?
Are you not/ aren´t you arriving?
Are they not/ aren´t they arriving?

10. To look at- mirar

POSITIVO (PRESENTE SIMPLE)	NEGATIVO
I look at	I do not/ don´t look at
You look at	You do not/ don´t look at
He/she/it looks at	He/ she/ it does not/ doesn´t look at
We look at	We do not/ don´t look at
You look at	You do not/ don´t look at
They look at	We do not/ don´t look at
POSITIVO (PRESENTE CONTINUO)	NEGATIVO
I am/ I´m looking at	I am / I´m not looking at
You are/ you´re looking at	You are not/ ´re not/ aren´t looking at
He/ she/ it is/´s looking at	He/she/it is not/ isn´t looking at
We are/ we´re looking at	We are not/ ´re not/ aren´t looking at
You are/ you´re looking at	You are not/ ´re not/ aren´t looking at
They are/ they´re looking at	They are not/ ´re not/ aren´t looking at

INTERROGATIVO (PRESENTE SIMPLE)
Do I/ do I not/ don´t I look at?
Do you/ do you not/ don´t you look at?
Does he/ she/ it not/ doesn´t he/she/ it look at?
Do we/ do we not/ don´t we
Do you/ do you not/ don´t you look at?
Do they/ do they not/ don´t they
INTERROGATIVO (PRESENTE CONTINUO)
Am I not/ aren´t I looking at
Are you not/ aren´t you looking at
Is he/she/it/ isn´t he she or it looking at
Are we not/ aren´t we looking at
Are you not/ aren´t you looking at
Are they not/ aren´t they looking at

11. To wear- llevar puesto

POSITIVO (PRESENTE SIMPLE)	NEGATIVO
I wear	I do not/ don´t wear
You wear	You do not/ don´t wear
He/ she/it wears	He/ she/ it does not/ doesn´t wear
We wear	We do not/ don´t wear
You wear	You do not/ don´t wear
They wear	They do not/ don´t wear
POSITIVO (PRESENTE CONTINUO)	NEGATIVO
I am/ I´m wearing	I am / I´m not wearing
You are/ you´re wearing	You are not/ ´re not/ aren´t wearing
He/ she/ it is/´s wearing	He/she/it is not/ isn´t wearing
We are/ we´re wearing	We are not/ ´re not/ aren´t wearing
You are/ you´re wearing	You are not/ ´re not/ aren´t wearing
They are/ they´re wearing	They are not/ ´re not/ aren´t wearing

INTERROGATIVO (PRESENTE SIMPLE)
Do I/ do I not/ don´t I wear
Do you/ do you not/ don´t you wear
Does he/ she/ it not/ doesn´t he/she/ it wear
Do we/ do we not/ don´t we wear
Do you/ do you not/ don´t you wear
Do they/ do they not/ don´t they wear
INTERROGATIVO (PRESENTE CONTINUO)
Am I not/ aren´t I wearing
Are you not/ aren´t you wearing
Is he/she/it/ isn´t he she or it wearing
Are we not/ aren´t we wearing
Are you not/ aren´t you wearing
Are they not/ aren´t they wearing

12. To practice- practicar

POSITIVO (PRESENTE SIMPLE)	NEGATIVO
I practice	I do not/ don´t practice
You practice	You do not/ don´t practice
He/she/it practices	He/ she/ it does not/ doesn´t practice
We practice	We do not/ don´t practice
You practice	You do not/ don´t practice
They practice	They do not/ don´t practice
POSITIVO (PRESENTE CONTINUO)	NEGATIVO
I am/ I´m practising	I am / I´m not practising
You are/ you´re practising	You are not/ ´re not/ aren´t practising
He/ she/ it is/´s practising	He/she/it is not/ isn´t practising
We are/ we´re practising	We are not/ ´re not/ aren´t practising
You are/ you´re practising	You are not/ ´re not/ aren´t practising
They are/ they´re practising	They are not/ ´re not/ aren´t practising

INTERROGATIVO (PRESENTE SIMPLE)
Do I/ do I not/ don´t I practice
Do you/ do you not/ don´t you practice
Does he/ she/ it not/ doesn´t he/she/ it practice
Do we/ do we not/ don´t we practice
Do you/ do you not/ don´t you practice
Do they/ do they not/ don´t they practice
INTERROGATIVO (PRESENTE CONTINUO)
Am I not/ aren´t I practising
Are you not/ aren´t you practising
Is he/she/it/ isn´t he she or it practising
Are we not/ aren´t we practising
Are you not/ aren´t you practising
Are they not/ aren´t they practising

13. To prepare- preparar

POSITIVO (PRESENTE SIMPLE)	NEGATIVO
I prepare	I do not/ don´t prepare
You prepare	You do not/ don´t prepare
He prepares	He/ she/ it does not/ doesn´t prepare
We prepare	We do not/ don´t prepare
You prepare	You do not/ don´t prepare
They prepare	They do not/ don´t prepare
POSITIVO (PRESENTE CONTINUO)	NEGATIVO
I am/ I´m preparing	I am / I´m not preparing
You are/ you´re preparing	You are not/ ´re not/ aren´t preparing
He/ she/ it is/´s preparing	He/she/it is not/ isn´t preparing
We are/ we´re preparing	We are not/ ´re not/ aren´t preparing
You are/ you´re preparing	You are not/ ´re not/ aren´t preparing
They are/ they´re preparing	They are not/ ´re not/ aren´t preparing

INTERROGATIVO (PRESENTE SIMPLE)
Do I/ do I not/ don´t I prepare?
Do you/ do you not/ don´t you prepare?
Does he/ she/ it not/ doesn´t he/she/ it prepare?
Do we/ do we not/ don´t we prepare?
Do you/ do you not/ don´t you prepare?
Do they/ do they not/ don´t they prepare?
INTERROGATIVO (PRESENTE CONTINUO)
Am I not/ aren´t I preparing?
Are you not/ aren´t you preparing?
Is he/she/it/ isn´t he she or it preparing?
Are we not/ aren´t we preparing?
Are you not/ aren´t you preparing?
Are they not/ aren´t they preparing?

14. To work- trabajar

POSITIVO (PRESENTE SIMPLE)	NEGATIVO
I work	I do not/ don´t work
You work	You do not/ don´t work
He/she/it works	He/ she/ it does not/ doesn´t work
We work	We do not/ don´t work
You work	You do not/ don´t work
They work	They do not/ don´t work
POSITIVO (PRESENTE CONTINUO)	NEGATIVO
I am/ I´m working	I am / I´m not working
You are/ you´re working	You are not/ ´re not/ aren´t working
He/ she/ it is/´s working	He/she/it is not/ isn´t working
We are/ you´re working	We are not/ ´re not/ aren´t working
You are/ you´re working	You are not/ ´re not/ aren´t working
They are/ you´re working	They are not/ ´re not/ aren´t working

INTERROGATIVO (PRESENTE SIMPLE)
Do I/ do I not/ don´t I work?
Do you/ do you not/ don´t you work?
Does he/ she/ it not/ doesn´t he/she/ it work?
Do we/ do we not/ don´t we work?
Do you/ do you not/ don´t you work?
Do they/ do they not/ don´t they work?
INTERROGATIVO (PRESENTE CONTINUO)
Am I not/ aren´t I working?
Are you not/ aren´t you working?
Is he/she/it/ isn´t he she or it working?
Are we not/ aren´t we working?
Are you not/ aren´t you working?
Are they not/ aren´t they working?

15. To play- Tocar/ jugar

POSITIVO (PRESENTE SIMPLE)	NEGATIVO
I play	I do not/ don´t play
You play	You do not/ don´t play
He/ she/ it plays	He/ she/ it does not/ doesn´t play
We play	We do not/ don´t play
You play	You do not/ don´t play
They play	They do not/ don´t play
POSITIVO (PRESENTE CONTINUO)	NEGATIVO
I am/ I´m playing	I am / I´m not playing
You are/ you´re playing	You are not/ ´re not/ aren´t playing
He/ she/ it is/´s playing	He/she/it is not/ isn´t playing
We are/ we´re playing	We are not/ ´re not/ aren´t playing
You are/ you´re playing	You are not/ ´re not/ aren´t playing
They are/ they´re playing	They are not/ ´re not/ aren´t playing

INTERROGATIVO (PRESENTE SIMPLE)
Do I/ do I not/ don´t I play?
Do you/ do you not/ don´t you play?
Does he/ she/ it not/ doesn´t he/she/ it play?
Do we/ do we not/ don´t we play?
Do you/ do you not/ don´t you play?
Do they/ do they not/ don´t they play?
INTERROGATIVO (PRESENTE CONTINUO)
Am I not/ aren´t I playing?
Are you not/ aren´t you playing?
Is he/she/it/ isn´t he she or it playing?
Are we not/ aren´t we playing?
Are you not/ aren´t you playing?
Are they not/ aren´t they playing?

PRACTICE B: (YouTube)

1. They play/ are playing/ 're playing the guitar.
2. She practices every day.
3. He prepares/ is preparing/ 's preparing the contract.
4. Chris wears/ is wearing trousers and a t- shirt..
5. I work/ I am/ I´m working in a bank.
6. We always sing in the bath.
7. You walk/ you are/ ´re walking to the school.
8. I dance every Saturday.
9. She looks for/is/´s looking for her dog.
10. We study/we are /´re studying Spanish at school.
11. I buy meat at the supermarket.
12. She listens to the radio every day.
13. You are/ ´re waiting for the bus.
14. I look at/I am/ I´m looking at the house.

PRACTICE C: (YouTube) *Ejemplos*

1. What do they play/What are/´re they playing?
2. When does she practice/ When is/´s she practising?
3. What does he prepare/ What is/´s he preparing?
4. What does/ What is/´s Carlos wearing?
5. Where do you work? /Where are/ ´re you working?
6. Where do you always sing?
7. Where do we walk to? Where are/´re we walking to?
8. When do you dance?
9. What is/ what´s she looking for?
10. Where do you study/ are you studying Spanish?
11. Where do you buy meat?
12. When does he listen to the radio?
13. What are/´re you waiting for?
14. What are/´re you looking at?
15. When do they arrive?/ When are/ ´re they arriving?

PRACTICE D: (YouTube) (free answers)

1. What languages do you speak?
2. When do you dance?
3. Do you sing karaoke?
4. Where do you study/ are you studying English?

5. When do you practice English?
6. Where do you work/ Where are you working?
7. How do you prepare a tortilla?
8. What music do you listen to/ are you listening to
9. Where do you buy clothes?
10. Are you looking for a new car?
11. What do you wear/ What are you wearing?
12. Do you walk/ Are you walking to work?
13. What instruments do you play?
14. When do you watch the televisión?

16. VERBOS DE "AR" EN CONTEXTO- "AR" VERBS IN CONTEXT

PRACTICA A:

VERBO	INFINITIVO	ESPAÑOL	PERSONA
1. are	To be	ser/ estar	3a persona plural
2. they are	To be	ser/ estar	3a persona plural
3. They are	To be	ser/ estar	3a persona plural
4. is studying	To study	estudiar	3a persona singular
5. is studying	To study	estudiar	3a persona singular
6. They study	To study	estudiar	3a persona plural
7. are	To be	ser/ estar	3a persona plural
8. speaks	To speak	hablar	3a persona singular
9. speaks	To speak	hablar	3a persona singular
10. practices	To practice	practicar	3a persona singular
11. speaks	To speak	hablar	3a persona singular
12. practices	To practice	practicar	3a persona singular
13. they both work	To work	trabajar	3a persona plural
14. works	To work	trabajar	3a persona singular
15. works	To work	trabajar	3a persona singular
16. They earn	To earn	ganar	3a persona plural
17. to buy	To buy	comprar	infinitive
18. to pay	To pay	pagar	infinitive
19. they walk	To walk	andar	3a persona plural
20. is	To be	ser/ estar	3a persona singular
21. they study	To study	estudiar	3a persona plural
22. they practice	To practice	practicar	3a persona plural

23. they watch	To watch	mirar	3a persona plural
24. John prepares	To prepare	preparar	3a persona singular
25. Susan plays	To play	tocar	3a persona singular
26. having dinner	To have dinner	cenar	infinitivo
27. they listen	To listen	escuchar	3a persona plural
28. speak	To speak	hablar	3a persona plural
29. to practice	To practice	practicar	infinitivo

PRACTICA B:

John y Susan son ingleses pero ahora están en España. Están en la Universidad de Madrid. John estudia español y María estudia español también. Estudian mucho y son muy buenos estudiantes.

Susan habla español perfectamente, y también habla francés, inglés y un poco de alemán. Practica todos los días en la universidad y con los amigos.
John habla español e inglés. Él practica mucho con los otros estudiantes y sus amigos.

Los sábados, los dos trabajan. John trabaja en una oficina y Susan trabaja en una tienda. Ganan dinero para comprar ropa y comida y pagar el alquiler. Todos los días andan a la Universidad. Su casa está muy cerca.

Por la tarde, después de las clases, estudian un poco. Practican el español con los amigos y luego miran la tele en casa. John prepara la cena y Susan toca la guitarra. Después de cenar, escuchan la radio, y hablan solamente en español para practicar más.

PRACTICA D:

1. Where are John and Susan from? John and Susan are English.
2. Where are they now? Now they are in Spain.
3. What does John study? /is John studying? John studies/ is studying Spanish.
4. Who studies/ is studying English also? Susan studies/ is studying English also.
5. What languages does Susan also speak? Susan also speaks French, English and a little German.
6. When does she practice? She practices every day.
7. Do they both work? Yes, they both work.
8. Who works in a shop? John works in a shop.
9. Why do they earn money? They earn money to buy clothes and food and to pay the rent.
10. How do they get to university? They walk to the university.

11. When do they watch the television? They watch the television at home.
12. Who prepares the dinner? John prepares the dinner.
13. What instrument does Susan play? Susan plays the guitar.
14. Why do they only speak in English? To practice more.

16. REGULAR VERBS - 2ND CONJUGATION – 'ER' VERBS

PRACTICE A: (YouTube)

1. To drink- beber

POSITIVO (PRESENTE SIMPLE)	NEGATIVO
I drink	I do not/ don´t drink
You drink	You do not/ don´t drink
He/ she/it drink	He/ she/ does not/ doesn´t drink
We drink	We do not/ don´t drink
You drink	You do not/ don´t drink
They drink	They do not/ don´t drink
POSITIVO (PRESENTE CONTINUO)	NEGATIVO
I am/ I´m drinking	I am not/ I´m not drinking?
You are/ you´re drinking	You are not/ you´re not/ you aren´t drinking
He/ she/it/´s drinking	He/she/it is not/isn´t drinking
we are/ we´re drinking	We are not/ we´re not/ we aren´t drinking
You are/ you´re drinking	You are not/ you´re not/ you aren´t drinking
they are/ they´re drinking	They are not/they´re not/they aren´t drinking

INTERROGATIVO (PRESENTE SIMPLE)
Do I / not/ don´t I drink?
Do you/not/don´t you drink?
Does he/ she/ it/not/ doesn´t he/ she/ it drink?
Do we/not/don´t we drink?
Do you/not/don´t you drink?
Do they/not/don´t they drink?
INTERROGATIVO (PRESENTE CONTINUO)
Am I/ not/ aren´t I drinking?
Are you/ not/ aren´t you drinking?
Is he/she/it/ not/ isn´t he/she/it drinking?
Are we/ not/ aren´t we drinking?
Are you/ not/ aren´t you drinking?
Are they/ not/ aren´t they drinking?

2. To learn- aprender

POSITIVO (PRESENTE SIMPLE)	NEGATIVO
I learn	I do not/ don´t learn
You learn	You do not/ don´t learn
He/ she/it learns	He/ she/ does not/ doesn´t learn
We learn	We do not/ don´t learn
You learn	You do not/ don´t learn
They learn	They do not/ don´t learn
POSITIVO (PRESENTE CONTINUO)	NEGATIVO
I am/ I´m learning	I am not/ I´m not learning
You are/ you´re learning	You are not/ you´re not/ you aren´t learning
He/ she/ it is/ ´s learning	He/ she/ it is/ isn´t learning
We are/ we´re learning	we are not/ we´re not/ you aren´t learning
You are/ you´re learning	You are not/ you´re not/ you aren´t learning
they are/ they´re learning	They are not/ they´re not/ you aren´t learning

INTERROGATIVO (PRESENTE SIMPLE)
Do I/not/don´t I learn?
Do you/not/don´t you learn?
Does he/ she/ it/not/ doesn´t he/ she/ it learn?
Do we/not/don´t we learn?
Do you/not/don´t you learn?
Do they/not/don´t they learn?
INTERROGATIVO (PRESENTE CONTINUO)
Am I/ not/ aren´t I learning?
Are you/ not/ aren´t you learning?
Is he/ she/it/ not/isn´t he/she/ it learning?
Are we/ not/ aren´t we learning?
Are you/ not/ aren´t you learning?
Are they/ not/ aren´t they learning?

3. To believe - creer

POSITIVO (PRESENTE SIMPLE)	NEGATIVO
I believe	I do not/ don´t believe
You believe	You do not/ don´t believe
He/ she/ it believes	He/ she/ does not/ doesn´t believe
We believe	We do not/ don´t believe
You believe	You do not/ don´t believe
They believe	They do not/ don´t believe
POSITIVO (PRESENTE CONTINUO)	NEGATIVO
I am/ I´m believing	I am not/ I´m not believing
You are/ you´re believing	You are not/you´re not/ you aren´t believing
He/ she/it is/´s believing	He/she/it is not/isn´t believing
We are/ we´re believing	We are not/we´re not/ we aren´t believing
You are/ you´re believing	You are not/you´re not/ you aren´t believing
They are/ they´re believing	They are not/they´re not/they aren´t believing

INTERROGATIVO (PRESENTE SIMPLE)
Do I/not/don´t I believe?
Do you/not/don´t you believe?
Does he/ she/ it/not/ doesn´t he/ she/ it believe?
Do we/not/don´t we believe?
Do you/not/don´t you believe?
Do they/not/don´t they believe?
INTERROGATIVO (PRESENTE CONTINUO)
Am I/not/aren´t I believing?
Are you/ not/ aren´t you believing?
Is he/she/it /not/ isn´t he/she/it believing?
Are we/ not/ aren´t we believing?
Are you/ not/ aren´t you believing?
Are they/ not/ aren´t they believing?

4. To sell- vender

POSITIVO (PRESENTE SIMPLE)	NEGATIVO
I sell	I do not/ don´t sell
You sell	You do not/ don´t sell
He/ she/it sells	He/ she/ does not/ doesn´t sell
We sell	We do not/ don´t sell
You sell	You do not/ don´t sell
They sell	We do not/ don´t sell
POSITIVO (PRESENTE CONTINUO)	NEGATIVO
I am/ I´m selling	I am/ I´m not selling
You are/ you´re selling	You are not/you´re not/ you aren´t selling
He/ she/ it is/ it´s selling	He/ she/ it is not/ isn´t selling
We are/ we´re selling	We are not/we´re not/ we aren´t selling
You are/ you´re selling	You are not/you´re not/ you aren´t selling
They are/ they´re selling	They are not/they´re not/ they aren´t selling

INTERROGATIVO (PRESENTE SIMPLE)
Do I/not/don´t I sell?
Do you/not/don´t you sell?
Does he/ she/ it/not/ doesn´t he/ she/ it sell?
Do we/not/don´t we sell?
Do you/not/don´t you sell?
Do they/not/don´t they sell?
INTERROGATIVO (PRESENTE CONTINUO)
Am I/ not/ aren´t I selling'
Are you/ not/ aren´t you selling'
Is he/ she/it/ not/isn´t he/she/it selling?
Are we/ not/ aren´t we selling?
Are you/ not/ aren´t you selling?
Are they/ not/ aren´t they selling?

5. To read- leer

POSITIVO (PRESENTE SIMPLE)	NEGATIVO
I read	I do not/ don´t read
You read	You do not/ don´t read
He/ she/ it reads	He/ she/ does not/ doesn´t read
we read	we do not/ don´t read
You read	You do not/ don´t read
They read	They do not/ don´t read
POSITIVO (PRESENTE CONTINUO)	NEGATIVO
I am/I´m reading	I am not/ I´m not reading
You are/ you´re reading	You are not/you´re not/ you aren´t reading
He/ she/ it is/´s reading	He/ she/ it is not/isn´t reading
We are/ we´re reading	We are not/we´re not/ we aren´t reading
You are/ you´re reading	You are not/you´re not/ you aren´t reading
They are/ they´re reading	They are not/they´re not/they aren´t reading

INTERROGATIVO (PRESENTE SIMPLE)
Do I / Do I not/ Don´t I read?
Do you / Do you not/ Don´t you read?
Does he/ she/ it/not/ doesn´t he/ she/ it read?
Do we / Do we not/ Don´t we read?
Do you / Do you not/ Don´t you read?
Do they / Do they not/ Don´t they read?
INTERROGATIVO (PRESENTE CONTINUO)
Am I / not/ aren´t I reading?
Are you/ not/ aren´t you reading?
Is he/ she/ it/ not/isn´t he/she/ it reading?
Are we/ not/ aren´t we reading?
Are you/ not/ aren´t you reading?
Are they/ not/ aren´t they reading?

6. To understand - comprender/ entender

POSITIVO (PRESENTE SIMPLE)	NEGATIVO
I understand	I do not/ don´t understand
You understand	You do not/ don´t understand
He/she/it understands	He/ she/ does not/ doesn´t understand
We understand	we do not/ don´t understand
You understand	You do not/ don´t understand
They understand	they do not/ don´t understand
POSITIVO (PRESENTE CONTINUO)	NEGATIVO
I am/ I´m understanding	I am not/ I´m not understanding
You are/ you´re understanding	You are not/´re not/aren´t understanding
He/ she/it is/´s understanding	He/she/it is not/ isn´t understanding
We are/ we´re understanding	We are not/´re not/aren´t understanding
You are/ you´re understanding	You are not/´re not/aren´t understanding
They are/ they´re understanding	They are not/´re not/aren´t understanding

INTERROGATIVO (PRESENTE SIMPLE)
Do I / Do I not/ Don´t I understand?
Do you / Do you not/ Don´t you understand?
Does he/ she/ it/ not/ doesn´t he/ she/ it understand?
Do we / Do we not/ Don´t we understand?
Do you / Do you not/ Don´t you understand?
Do they / Do they not/ Don´t they understand?
INTERROGATIVO (PRESENTE CONTINUO)
Am I/not/aren´t I understanding?
Are you/ not/ aren´t you understanding?
Isn´t he/ she/it understanding?
Are we/ not/ aren´t we understanding?
Are you/ not/ aren´t you understanding?
Are they/ not/ aren´t they understanding?

7. To run- correr

POSITIVO (PRESENTE SIMPLE)	NEGATIVO
I run	I do not/ don´t run
You run	You do not/ don´t run
He/ she/it runs	He/ she/ does not/ doesn´t run
We run	We do not/ don´t run
You run	You do not/ don´t run
They run	They do not/ don´t run
POSITIVO (PRESENTE CONTINUO)	NEGATIVO
I am/I´m running	I am not/ I´m not running
You are/ you´re running	You are not/´re not/aren´t running
He/she/ it is/´s running	He/ she/ it is not/isn't running
We are/ you´re running	We are not/´re not/aren´t running
You are/ you´re running	You are not/´re not/aren´t running
they are/ they´re running	They are not/´re not/aren´t running

INTERROGATIVO (PRESENTE SIMPLE)
Do I / Do I not/ Don´t I run?
Do you / Do you not/ Don´t you run?
Does he/ she/ it not/ doesn´t he/she/ it run?
Do we/ Do we not/ Don´t we run?
Do you / Do you not/ Don´t you run?
Do they / Do they not/ Don´t they run?
INTERROGATIVO (PRESENTE CONTINUO)
Am I /not/ aren´t I running?
Are you/ not/ aren´t you running?
Is he/she/it/ not/ isn´t he/ she/ it running?
Are we/ not/ aren´t we running?
Are you/ not/ aren´t you running?
Are they/ not/ aren´t they running?

8. To cough - toser

POSITIVO (PRESENTE SIMPLE)	NEGATIVO
I cough	I do not/ don´t cough
You cough	You do not/ don´t cough
He/she/ it cough	He/ she/ does not/ doesn´t cough
We cough	You do not/ don´t cough
You cough	You do not/ don´t cough
They cough	You do not/ don´t cough
POSITIVO (PRESENTE CONTINUO)	NEGATIVO
I am/I´m coughing	I am not/ I.m not coughing
You are/ you´re coughing	You are not/´re not/aren´t coughing
He/she/ it is/´s coughing	He/she/it is not/isn´t coughing
We are/ we´re coughing	We are not/´re not/aren´t coughing
You are/ you´re coughing	You are not/´re not/aren´t coughing
They are/ they´re coughing	They are not/´re not/aren´t coughing

INTERROGATIVO (PRESENTE SIMPLE)
Do you / Do you not/ Don´t you cough?
Do you / Do you not/ Don´t you cough?
Does he/ she/ it not/ doesn´t he/she/ it cough?
Do we / Do we not/ Don´t we cough?
Do you / Do you not/ Don´t you cough?
Do they/ Do they not/ Don´t they cough?
INTERROGATIVO (PRESENTE CONTINUO)
Am I /not/ aren´t I coughing?
Are you/ not/ aren´t you coughing?
Is he/ she/ it notI isn´t he/ she it coughing?
Are we/ not/ aren´t we coughing?
Are you/ not/ aren´t you coughing?
Are they/ not/ aren´t they coughing?

9. To break- romper

POSITIVO (PRESENTE SIMPLE)	NEGATIVO
I break	I do not/ don´t break
You break	You do not/ don´t break
He/ she/it break	He/ she/ does not/ doesn´t break
We break	We do not/ don´t break
You break	You do not/ don´t break
They break	They do not/ don´t break
POSITIVO (PRESENTE CONTINUO)	NEGATIVO
I am/I´m breaking	I am not/ I´m not breaking
You are/ you´re breaking	You are not/´re not/aren´t breaking
He/ she/it is not/ isn´t breaking	He/she/it is not/ isn´t breaking
We are/ we´re breaking	We are not/´re not/aren´t breaking
You are/ you´re breaking	You are not/´re not/aren´t breaking
They are/ they´re breaking	They are not/´re not/aren´t breaking

INTERROGATIVO (PRESENTE SIMPLE)
Do I/not/don´t I break?
Do you/not/don´t you break?
Does he/ she/ it not/ doesn´t he/she/ it break?
Do we/not/don´t we break?
Do you/not/don´t you break?
Do they/not/don´t they break?
INTERROGATIVO (PRESENTE CONTINUO)
Am I/not/aren´t I breaking?
Are you/ not/ aren´t you breaking?
Is he/she/it/ not/ isn´t he/ she/ it breaking?
Are we/ not/ aren´t we breaking?
Are you/ not/ aren´t you breaking?
Are they/ not/ aren´t they breaking?

10. To see- ver

POSITIVO (PRESENTE SIMPLE)	NEGATIVO
I see	I do not/ don´t see
You see	You do not/ don´t see
He/ she/ it sees	He/ she/ does not/ doesn´t see
We see	We do not/ don´t see
You see	You do not/ don´t see
They see	They do not/ don´t see
POSITIVO (PRESENTE CONTINUO)	NEGATIVO
I am/I´m seeing	I am not/I´m not seeing
You are/ you´re seeing	You are not/´re not/aren´t seeing
He/ she/it is/´s seeing	He is not/ isn´t seeing
We are/ we´re seeing	We are not/´re not/aren´t seeing
You are/ you´re seeing	You are not/´re not/aren´t seeing
They are/ they´re seeing	They are not/´re not/aren´t seeing

INTERROGATIVO (PRESENTE SIMPLE)
Do I/not/don´t I see?
Do you/not/don´t you see?
Does he/ she/ it not/ doesn´t he/she/ it see?
Do we/not/don´t we see?
Do you/not/don´t you see?
Do they/not/don´t they see?
INTERROGATIVO (PRESENTE CONTINUO)
Am I/not/ aren´t I seeing?
Are you/ not/ aren´t you seeing?
Is he/she/it/not/isn´t he/she/it seeing?
Are we/ not/ aren´t we seeing?
Are you/ not/ aren´t you seeing?
Are they/ not/ aren´t they seeing?

PRACTICE B: (YouTube)

1. I often eat in an English restaurant.
2. I drink milk every day.
3. He doesn´t understand Russian.

4. We read a lot of books.
5. You learn/ are learning a lot of English on the Internet.
6. Mark sells/ is selling clothes at the market.
7. Mary always runs in the marathon.
8. Many Americans understand Spanish.
9. We beliieve in UFOs.
10. They always cough in the morning.
11. Are you learning English?
12. I break something every day.
13. She watches a lot on Netflix at the weekends.
14. We always drink beer in the bar.
15. You eat a lot of vegetables.
16. They normally sell cars but in summer they sell houses.

PRACTICE C: (YouTube) (free answers)

1. What do you see from your bedroom window?
2. Why do you study/ are you studying English?
3. Do you understand English verbs?
4. What do you drink in a restaurant?
5. Do you believe in ghosts?
6. Are you selling your house?
7. Do you break many things?
8. Do you read a lot of books?
9. Where do you normally eat on a Sunday?
10. Do smokers cough more than non- smokers?
11. Do you eat vegetables?
12. When do you drink alcohol in the house?
13. When do you run?
14. Do you learn better in the morning or at night?
15. Why do you drink wáter in the summer?

18. VERBOS REGULARES "ER" EN CONTEXTO- "ER" VERBS IN CONTEXT

PRACTICA A:

VERBO EN CONTEXTO	INFINITIVO	ESPAÑOL	PERSONA
1. are	To be	Estar	3a p. plural
2. is drinking	To drink	Beber	3a p. sing
3. is drinking	To drink	Beber	3a p. sing
4. is reading	To read	leer	3a p. sing
5. is reading	To read	leer	3a p. sing
6. they understand	To understand	comprender/ entender	3a p. plural
7. they learn	To learn	aprender	3a p. plural
8. they also learn	To learn	aprender	3a p. plural
9. they read	To read	leer	3a p. plural
10. they watch	To watch	Ver/ mirar	3a p. plural
11. they believe	To believe	creer	3a p. plural
12. is	To be	ser	3a p. sing
13. sees	To see	ver	3a p. sing
14. is selling	To sell	vender	3a p. sing
15. believe	To believe	creer	3a p. plural
16. they need	To need	necesitar	3a p. plural
17. to buy	To buy	comprar	infinitive
18. to do	To do	hacer	infinitive
19. they both eat	To eat	comer	3a p. plural
20. eats	To eat	comer	3a p. sing
21. eats	To eat	comer	3a p. sing
22. eats	To eat	comer	3a p. sing
23. eats	To eat	comer	3a p. sing
24. having lunch	To have lunch	comer	"ing"
25. they both drink	To drink	beber	3a p. plural
26. They finish	To finish	terminar	3a p. plural
27. having lunch	To have lunch	comer	"ing"
28. they pay	To pay	pagar	3a p. plural
29. breaks	To break	romper	3a p. sing
30. is	To be	estar	3a p. sing
31. isn´t	To be	estar	3a psing
32. they both run	To run	correr	3a p. plural
33. it´s	To be	ser	3a p. sing
34. they need	To need	necesitar	3a p. plural
35. to catch	To catch	coger	infinitive

TRANSLATION:

John y Susan *están* en un restaurante español en el centro de la ciudad de Madrid.

Susan bebe vino tinto y John bebe cerveza. Susan lee una revista y John lee un periódico. Comprenden muchas de las palabras españolas pero no todas.

Aprenden mucho español con sus amigos españoles, pero también aprenden mucho cuando leen periódicos y revistas, y cuando ven la tele por la noche. Creen que el español es muy importante para su futuro.

John ve un anuncio en el periódico, un chico vende una bicicleta. Los dos creen que deben comprar esta bicicleta para hacer más ejercicio.

De primero, los dos comen ensalada. De segundo, Susan come paella y John come macarrones. De postre, John come flan y Susan come arroz con leche. Después de comer, los dos beben café con leche.

Terminan de comer a las cuatro más o menos. Cuando pagan la cuenta, John rompe un vaso que está en la mesa. El camarero no está enfadado, y los dos corren a la parada del autobús porque ahora es tarde y deben coger el autobús a las cuatro y cuarto.

PRACTICA B: (YouTube)

1. Where are John and Susan? They are in a Spanish restaurant in Madrid city centre.
2. What is Susan drinking? Susan is drinking red wine.
3. Who is drinking beer? John is drinking beer.
4. What are they reading? Susan is reading a magazine and John is reading a newspaper.
5. When do they learn a lot of Spanish? They learn a lot of Spanish with their Spanish friends.
6. Why do they believe that Spanish is very important? They believe that Spanish is very important for their future?
7. What does John see in the newspaper? John sees an advert in the newspaper.
8. What is/´s the boy selling? The boy is/´s selling a bicycle.
9. Why do they need to buy this bicycle? They need to buy this bicycle to do more exercise.
10. What do they both eat for starter/ first course? They both eat salad.
11. Who eats paella for main course? Susan eats paella for main/ second course.
12. What does John eat for pudding/ dessert? John eats flan for pudding/dessert.
13. What do they both drink after having lunch? They both drink coffee with milk.

14. What time do they finish having lunch? They finish having lunch at around four o´clock.
15. What does John break when they pay the bill? John breaks a glass that is on the table.
16. Is the waiter angry? No, the waiter is not/ isn´t angry.
17. Why do they run to the bus stop? Because now it is/ it´s late
18. What time do they need to catch the bus? They need to catch the bus at quarter past four.

19. REGULAR VERBS - 3RD CONJUGATION – 'IR' VERBS

PRACTICE A: (YouTube)

1. to write- escribir

POSITIVO (PRESENTE SIMPLE)	NEGATIVO
I write	I do not/ don´t write
You write	You do not/ don´t write
He/ she/ it writes	He/she/it does not/doesn´t write
We write	we do not/ don´t write
You write	You do not/ don´t write
They write	they do not/ don´t write
POSITIVO (PRESENTE CONTINUO)	NEGATIVO
I am/´m writing	I am/´m not writing
You are/´re writing	You are/´re/not/aren´t writing
He/she/it/is/´s writing	He/she/it/is/´s/not/isn´t writing
We are/´re writing	We are/´re/not/aren´t writing
You are/´re writing	You are/´re/not/aren´t writing
They are/´re writing	They are/´re/not/aren´t writing

INTERROGATIVO (PRESENTE SIMPLE)
Do I/ not/ don´t I write?
Do you/ not/ don´t you write?
Does he/she/it/not/ doesn´t he/ she/it write?
Do we/ not/ don´t we write?
Do you/ not/ don´t you write?
Do they/ not/ don´t they write?
INTERROGATIVO (PRESENTE CONTINUO)
Am I /not/ aren´t I writing?
Are you/ not/ aren´t you writing?
Is/he/she/it/ not/ isn´t he/ she/ it writing?
Are we/ not/ aren´t we writing?
Are you/ not/ aren´t you writing?
Are they/ not/ aren´t they writing?

2. to receive - recibir

POSITIVO (PRESENTE SIMPLE)	NEGATIVO
I receive	I do not/ don´t receive
You receive	You do not/ don´t receive
He/she/it receives	He/she/it does not/doesn´t receive
We receive	We do not/ don´t receive
You receive	You do not/ don´t receive
They receive	They do not/ don´t receive
POSITIVO (PRESENTE CONTINUO)	NEGATIVO
I am/´m receiving	I am/´m not receiving
You are/´re/receiving	You are/´re/not/aren´t receiving
He/she/it/is/´s receiving	He/she/it/is/´s/not/isn´t receiving
We are/´re receiving	We are/´re/not/aren´t receiving
You are/´re/receiving	You are/´re/not/aren´t receiving
They are/´re receiving	They are/´re/not/aren´t receiving

INTERROGATIVO (PRESENTE SIMPLE)
Do I/ not/ don´t I receive?
Do you/ not/ don´t you receive?
Does he/she/it/not/ doesn´t he/ she/it receive?
Do we/ not/ don´t we receive?
Do you/ not/ don´t you receive?
Do you/ not/ don´t you receive?
INTERROGATIVO (PRESENTE CONTINUO)
Am I /not/ aren´t I receiving?
Are you/ not/ aren´t you receiving?
Is/he/she/it/ not/ isn´t he/ she/ it receiving?
Are we/ not/ aren´t you receiving?
Are you/ not/ aren´t you receiving?
Are they/ not/ aren´t they receiving?

3. to cover- cubrir

POSITIVO (PRESENTE SIMPLE)	NEGATIVO
I cover	I do not/ don´t cover
You cover	You do not/ don´t cover
He/she/ it covers	He/she/it does not/doesn´t cover
We cover	We do not/ don´t cover
You cover	You do not/ don´t cover
They cover	They do not/ don´t cover
POSITIVO (PRESENTE CONTINUO)	NEGATIVO
I am/´m covering	I am/´m not covering
You are/´re covering	You are/´re/not/aren´t covering
He/she/it is/´s covering	He/she/it is/´s/ not/ isn´t covering
We are/´re covering	We are/´re/not/aren´t covering
You are/´re covering	You are/´re/not/aren´t covering
They are/´re covering	They are/´re/not/aren´t covering

INTERROGATIVO (PRESENTE SIMPLE)
Do I/ not/ don´t I cover?
Do you/ not/ don´t you cover?
Does he/she/it/not/ doesn´t he/ she/it cover?
Do we/ not/ don´t we cover?
Do you/ not/ don´t you cover?
Do they/ not/ don´t they cover?
INTERROGATIVO (PRESENTE CONTINUO)
Am I /not/ aren´t I covering?
Are you/ not/ aren´t you covering?
Is/he/she/it/ not/ isn´t he/ she/ it covering?
Are we/ not/ aren´t we covering?
Are you/ not/ aren´t you covering?
Are they/ not/ aren´t they covering?

4. To get on- subir

POSITIVO (PRESENTE SIMPLE)	NEGATIVO
I get on	I do not/ don´t get on
You get on	You do not/ don´t get on
He/ she/ it gets on	He/she/it does not/doesn´t get on
We get on	We do not/ don´t get on
You get on	You do not/ don´t get on
We get on	They do not/ don´t get on
POSITIVO (PRESENTE CONTINUO)	NEGATIVO
I am/´m getting on	I am/´m not getting on
You are/ ´re getting on	You are/ ´re not/ aren´t getting on
He/she/it is/´s getting on	He/she/it/is/´s/not/isn´t getting on
We are/ ´re getting on	We are/ ´re not/ aren´t getting on
You are/ ´re getting on	You are/ ´re not/ aren´t getting on
They are/ ´re getting on	They are/ ´re not/ aren´t getting on

INTERROGATIVO (PRESENTE SIMPLE)
Do I/ not/ don´t I get on?
Do you/ not/ don´t you get on?
Does he/she/it/not/ doesn´t he/ she/it get on?
Do we/ not/ don´t we get on?
Do you/ not/ don´t you get on?
Do they/ not/ don´t they get on?
INTERROGATIVO (PRESENTE CONTINUO)
Am I /not/ aren´t I getting on?
Are you/ not/ aren´t you getting on?
Is/he/she/it/ not/ isn´t he/ she/ it getting on?
Are we/ not/ aren´t we getting on?
Are you/ not/ aren´t you getting on?
Are they/ not/ aren´t they getting on?

5. to discover- descubrir

POSITIVO (PRESENTE SIMPLE)	NEGATIVO
I discover	I do not/ don´t discover
You discover	You do not/ don´t discover
He/ she/ it discovers	He/ she/it does not/doesn´t discover
We discover	We do not/ don´t discover
You discover	You do not/ don´t discover
They discover	They do not/ don´t discover
POSITIVO (PRESENTE CONTINUO)	NEGATIVO
I am/´m discovering	I am/´m not discovering
You are/ ´re discovering	You are/ ´re not/ aren´t discovering
He/she/it is/´s discovering	He/she/it/is/´s/not/isn´t discovering
We are/ ´re discovering	We are/ ´re not/ aren´t discovering
You are/ ´re discovering	You are/ ´re not/ aren´t discovering
They are/ ´re discovering	They are/ ´re not/ aren´t discovering

INTERROGATIVO (PRESENTE SIMPLE)
Do I/ not/ don´t I discover?
Do you/ not/ don´t you discover?
Does he/she/it/not/ doesn´t he/ she/it discover?
Do we/ not/ don´t we discover?
Do you/ not/ don´t you discover?
Do they/ not/ don´t they discover?
INTERROGATIVO (PRESENTE CONTINUO)
Am I /not/ aren´t I discovering?
Are you/ not/ aren´t you discovering?
Is/he/she/it/ not/ isn´t he/ she/ it discovering?
Are we/ not/ aren´t we discovering?
Are you/ not/ aren´t you discovering?
Are they/ not/ aren´t they discovering?

6. to share- compartir

POSITIVO (PRESENTE SIMPLE)	NEGATIVO
I share	I do not/ don´t share
You share	You do not/ don´t share
He/ she/it shares	He/she/it does not/doesn´t share
We share	We do not/ don´t share
You share	You do not/ don´t share
They share	They do not/ don´t share
POSITIVO (PRESENTE CONTINUO)	NEGATIVO
I am/´m sharing	I am/´m not sharing
You are/ ´re sharing	You are/ ´re not/ aren´t sharing
He/ she/ it is´s sharing	He/she/it/is/´s/not/isn´t sharing
We are/ ´re sharing	We are/ ´re not/ aren´t sharing
You are/ ´re sharing	You are/ ´re not/ aren´t sharing
They are/ ´re sharing	They are/ ´re not/ aren´t sharing

INTERROGATIVO (PRESENTE SIMPLE)
Do I/ not/ don´t I share?
Do you/ not/ don´t you share?
Does he/she/it/not/ doesn´t he/ she/it share?
Do we/ not/ don´t we share?
Do you/ not/ don´t you share?
Do they/ not/ don´t they share?
INTERROGATIVO (PRESENTE CONTINUO)
Am I /not/ aren´t I sharing?
Are you/ not/ aren´t you sharing?
Is/he/she/it/ not/ isn´t he/ she/ it sharing?
Are we/ not/ aren´t we sharing?
Are you/ not/ aren´t you sharing
Are they/ not/ aren´t they sharing?

7. to suffer- sufrir

POSITIVO (PRESENTE SIMPLE)	NEGATIVO
I suffer	I do not/ don´t suffer
You suffer	You do not/ don´t suffer
He/ she/ it suffers	He/she/it does not/ doesn´t suffer
We suffer	We do not/ don´t suffer
You suffer	You do not/ don´t suffer
They suffer	They do not/ don´t suffer
POSITIVO (PRESENTE CONTINUO)	NEGATIVO
I am/´m suffering	I am/´m not suffering
You are/ ´re suffering	You are/ ´re not/ aren´t suffering
He/she/it is/´s suffering	He/she/it/is/´s/not/isn´t suffering
We are/ ´re suffering	We are/ ´re not/ aren´t suffering
You are/ ´re suffering	You are/ ´re not/ aren´t suffering
They are/ ´re suffering	They are/ ´re not/ aren´t suffering

INTERROGATIVO (PRESENTE SIMPLE)
Do I/ not/ don´t I suffer?
Do you/ not/ don´t you suffer?
Does he/she/it/not/ doesn´t he/ she/it suffer?
Do we/ not/ don´t we suffer?
Do you/ not/ don´t you suffer?
Do they/ not/ don´t they suffer?
INTERROGATIVO (PRESENTE CONTINUO)
Am I /not/ aren´t I suffering?
Are you/ not/ aren´t you suffering?
Is/he/she/it/ not/ isn´t he/ she/ it suffering?
Are we/ not/ aren´t we suffering?
Are you/ not/ aren´t you suffering?
Are they/ not/ aren´t they suffering?

8. to hand out - repartir

POSITIVO (PRESENTE SIMPLE)	NEGATIVO
I hand out	I do not/ don´t
You hand out	You do not/ don´t
He/ she/it hands out	He/she/it does not/ doesn´t
We hand out	We do not/ don´t
They hand out	You do not/ don´t
We hand out	They do not/ don´t
POSITIVO (PRESENTE CONTINUO)	NEGATIVO
I am/´m handing out	I am/´m not handing out
You are/ ´re handing out	You are/ ´re not/ aren´t handing out
He/she/it is/´s handing out	He/she/it/is/´s/not/isn´t handing out
We are/ ´re handing out	We are/ ´re not/ aren´t handing out
You are/ ´re handing out	You are/ ´re not/ aren´t handing out
They are/ ´re handing out	They are/´re not/ aren´t handing out

INTERROGATIVO (PRESENTE SIMPLE)
Do I/ not/ don´t I hand out?
Do you/ not/ don´t you hand out?
Does he/she/it/not/ doesn´t he/ she/it hand out?
Do we/ not/ don´t we hand out?
Do you/ not/ don´t you hand out?
Do they/ not/ don´t they hand out?
INTERROGATIVO (PRESENTE CONTINUO)
Am I /not/ aren´t I handing out?
Are you/ not/ aren´t you handing out?
Is/he/she/it/ not/ isn´t he/ she/ it handing out?
Are we/ not/ aren´t we handing out?
Are you/ not/ aren´t you handing out?
Are they/ not/ aren´t they handing out?

9. To open- abrir

POSITIVO (PRESENTE SIMPLE)	NEGATIVO
I open	I do not/ don´t open
You open	You do not/ don´t open
He/ she/ it opens	He/she/it does not/ doesn´t open
We open	We do not/ don´t open
You open	You do not/ don´t open
They open	they do not/ don´t open
POSITIVO (PRESENTE CONTINUO)	NEGATIVO
I am/´m opening	I am/´m not opening
You are/ ´re opening	You are/ ´re not/ aren´t opening
He/she/it is not/isn´t opening	He/she/it/is/´s/not/isn´t opening
We are/ ´re opening	We are/ ´re not/ aren´t opening
You are/ ´re opening	You are/ ´re not/ aren´t opening
They are/ ´re opening	They are/ ´re not/ aren´t opening

INTERROGATIVO (PRESENTE SIMPLE)
Do I/ not/ don´t I open?
Do you/ not/ don´t you open?
Does he/she/it/not/ doesn´t he/ she/it open?
Do we/ not/ don´t we open?
Do you/ not/ don´t you open?
Do they/ not/ don´t they open?
INTERROGATIVO (PRESENTE CONTINUO)
Am I /not/ aren´t I opening?
Are you/ not/ aren´t you opening?
Is/he/she/it/ not/ isn´t he/ she/ it opening?
Are we/ not/ aren´t we opening?
Are you/ not/ aren´t you opening?
Are they/ not/ aren´t they opening?

10. To argue- discutir

POSITIVO (PRESENTE SIMPLE)	NEGATIVO
I argue	I do not/ don´t argue
You argue	You do not/ don´t argue
He/ she/ it argues	He/she/it does not/ doesn´t argue
We argue	We do not/ don´t argue
You argue	You do not/ don´t argue
They argue	They do not/ don´t argue
POSITIVO (PRESENTE CONTINUO)	NEGATIVO
I am/´m arguing	I am/´m not arguing
You are/ ´re arguing	You are/ ´re not/ aren´t arguing
He/she/it/is/´s arguing	He/she/it/is/´s/not/isn´t arguing
We are/ ´re arguing	We are/ ´re not/ aren´t arguing
You are/´re arguing	You are/ ´re not/ aren´t arguing
They are/ ´re arguing	They are/ ´re not/ aren´t arguing

INTERROGATIVO (PRESENTE SIMPLE)
Do I/ not/ don´t I argue?
Do you/ not/ don´t you argue?
Does he/she/it/not/ doesn´t he/ she/it argue?
Do we/ not/ don´t we argue?
Do you/ not/ don´t you argue?
Do they/ not/ don´t they argue?
INTERROGATIVO (PRESENTE CONTINUO)
Am I /not/ aren´t I arguing?
Are you/ not/ aren´t you arguing?
Is/he/she/it/ not/ isn´t he/ she/ it arguing?
Are we/ not/ aren´t we arguing?
Are you/ not/ aren´t you arguing?
Are they/ not/ aren´t they arguing?

PRACTICA B:

1. Do you write many emails?
2. In Africa, many children suffer/ are suffering.

3. The snow covers/ is covering the mountains.
4. I get on/ am getting on the train in Barcelona.
5. We always discover the truth in the end.
6. The teacher hands out/ is handing out the exams.
7. Jack and Peter share/ are sharing a flat/ an apartment in Madrid.
8. Do you receive a lot of letters?
9. He always opens the doors for me.
10. They argue every Saturday night.
11. Do they not/ don´t they/ live/are they not/ aren´t they living in Madrid?
12. Do you write/ are you writing in English or Spanish?
13. Does she open/ is she opening the shop?
14. The postman hands out/ is handing out the post.
15. Don´t we get on/ are we not/ aren´t we getting on the train in Alicante?
16. We do not/ don´t/ are not/aren´t arguing just talk/ talking.
17. I share everything with my family.
18. What time do I get on/ am I getting on the train?
19. We do not/don´t cover the garden furniture.
20. When do you discover the truth?
21. I suffer/ am/ ´m suffering a lot because of bad neighbours.
22. She does not/ doesn´t receive/ is not/ isn´t receiving post.
23. Does the tablecloth cover the table?
24. Fran is arguing with her again.
25. They do not/ don´t/ open/ are not/ aren´t opening until the 4th June.

20. TRANSLATION FROM ENGLISH TO SPANISH -REGULAR VERBS

PRACTICE A: verbs

1. vive
2. works
3. studies
4. watches
5. speaks
6. He doesn´t understand
7. reads
8. visits
9. drinks
10. come
11. vende
12. escribe

13. aprende
14. es
15. tiene
16. es
17. comparte

PRACTICE B: (YouTube)

Mark lives in Benidorm with his family. He Works in a shop, and on Wednesday evenings he studies Spanish in a private school.
He watches the televisión on Mondays and on Tuesdays he speaks/talks to his Spanish friends. HHe doesn´t understand everything.
On Thursdays he reads history books, and on Fridays he visits a local bar. He always drinks beer and eats fish and chips. On Saturdays he sells clothes at the market, and on Sundays he writes emails to his Spanish friends. He learns a lot of Spanish with them.
Mark is tall, dark and has brown eyes. He is very nice and shares everything with his family.

PRACTICE C: (YouTube)

1. Where does Mark live/ is Mark living and who with? Mark lives/ is living in Benidorm with his family.
2. Where does he workI is he working? He works/ is working in a shop.
3. What does he study/ is he studying on Wednesday evenings? He studies/ is studying English.
4. Where does he/ is he studying? He studies/ is studying in a private school.
5. What does he do on Mondays? He watches the television on Mondays.
6. Who does he speak/ talk to on Tuesdays? He speaks/ talks to his Spanish friends.
7. Does he understand everything? No, he does not/ doesn´t understand everything.
8. What does he read on Thursdays? On Thursdays he reads history books
9. What does he also eat and drink in his local bar on Fridays. He always drinks beer and eats fish and chips.
10. What does he sell at the market on Saturdays? On Saturdays he sells clothes.
11. Who does he write to on Sundays? He writes emails to his Spanish friends.
12. What is Mark like? He is/ He´s very nice and shares everything with his family.

21. ADVERBS OF FREQUENCY

PRACTICE A: (YouTube)

1. Always
2. A menudo
3. Normally
4. Sometimes
5. Almost never
6. Never
7. Once in a while
8. Once a week
9. Once a month
10. Once a year
11. Every day
12. Every week
13. Every month
14. Every Saturday
15. Every morning
16. Every afternoon/ evening

PRACTICE B: (free answers)

22. PRACTICAR VERBOS REGULARES- PRACTICE OF REGULAR VERBS

PRACTICA B:

	VERBO IN CONTEXTO	INFINITIVO	ESPAÑOL	CONTEXTO	PERSONA
1	is	To be	ser	es	3a p. singular
2	We live	To live	vivir	vivimos	1a p. plural
3	works	To work	trabajar	trabaja	3a p. singular
4	works	To work	trabajar	trabaja	3a p. singular
5	They work	To work	trabajar	trabajan	3a p.plural
6	leaves	To leave	salir	sale	3a p. singular
7	catches	To catch	coger	coge	3a p. singular
8	catches	To catch	coger	coge	3a p. singular
9	study	To study	estudiar	estudio	1a persona sing

10	come home	To come home	Regresar a casa	Regreso a casa	1a persona sing
11	I have lunch	To have lunch	comer	como	1a p. singular
12	Have lunch	To have lunch	comer	comen	3a p. plural
13	Doesn´t work	To work	trabajar	No trabaja	3a p. singular
14	tidies	To tidy	ordenar	ordena	3a p. singular
15	prepares	To prepare	preparar	prepara	3a p. singular
16	washes	To wash	lavar	lava	3a p. singular
17	irons	To iron	planchar	plancha	3a p. singular
18	We help	To help	ayudar	ayuda	1a p. plural
19	She rests	To rest	descansar	descansa	3a p. singular
20	We return home	To return home	Regresar a casa	Regresamos a casa	1a p. plural
21	reads	To read	leer	lee	3a p. singular
22	watches	To watch	Mirar/ ver	Mira/ ve	3a p. singular
23	reads	To read	leer	lee	3a p. singular
24	sings	To sing	cantar	canta	3a p. singular
25	Doesn´t have dinner	To have dinner	cenar	cena	3a p. singular
26	Having dinner	To have dinner	cenar	cena	"ing"- infinitive
27	I study	To study	estudiar	estudio	1a p. singular
28	watch	To watch	Mirar/ ver	Miran/ ven	3a p. plural
28	listen	To listen	escuchar	escuchan	3a p. plural
28	prepare	To prepare	preparar	preparan	3a p. plural

PRACTICA C:

Mi nombre es Paul Smith. Vivimos en Manchester, a 6, Barlow Terrace. Mi padre trabaja en un banco y mi madre trabaja en un hospital. Trabajan de lunes a viernes. My padre sale de la casa a las ocho y mi madre a las nueve. My padre coge el autobús y mi madre coge el tren.

Estudio español en la universidad. Nunca regreso a casa a mediodía. Como/almuerzo en el comedor en el campus con mis compañeros de clase. Mis padres comen/ almuerzan en el trabajo.

Mi hermana no trabaja hasta la tarde/ noche. Ordena la casa, prepara las comidas, lava la ropa o plancha. Ayudamos con todo esto los fines de semanas y ella descansa.

Regresamos a casa sobre las cinco o seis. Mi padre lee el periódico, mi madre mira/ve la televisión o lee un libro. Mi hermana canta en un bar cerca la casa y no cena con nosotros. Muchas veces, después de cenar, estudio hasta las doce/ medionoche. Mis padres miran/ ven la televisión, escuchan la radio o preparan cosas para la mañana.

PRACTICA D: (YouTube)

1. Where does Paul Smith and his family live? They live in Manchester.
2. Where do his mother and father work? His father works in a bank and his mother works in a hospital.
3. What/ which days do they work? They work Monday to Friday.
4. What time do they leave the house? His father leaves the house at eight a.m and his mother at 9 a.m.
5. What does his father catch? His father catches the bus.
6. And his mother? His mother catches the train.
7. Does Paul work? No, he doesn´t work.
8. What does he study? /What is he studying?
9. Where does he study/ Where is he studying?
10. Does he come back/ return to the house at midday?
11. Where does he have lunch? He has lunch in the dining room at the campus with his classmates.
12. Where do his parents have lunch? They have lunch at work.
13. Does his sister work? Yes, she works in the evening.
14. What does she do in the house? She tidies the house, prepares the meals, washes the clothes or irons
15. What time do they come back/ return home? They come back/ return home at 5 or 6 p.m.
16. What do his mother and father do then? His father reads the paper and his mother watches the television or reads a book.
17. Where does his sister sing? She sings in a bar near to the house.
18. Does she have dinner with them? No, she doesn´t have dinner with them.
19. What does Paul do then? Often he studies until midnight.
20. What do his parents do? They watch the television, listen to the radio or prepare things for the morning.

21. DIPTHONGS - ROOT OR STEM CHANGING VERBS

DIPTHONGS 1 - PRACTICE A: (YouTube)

1. To sleep - dormir

POSITIVO (PRESENTE SIMPLE)	NEGATIVO
I sleep	I do/ not/ don´t sleep
You sleep	I do/ not/ don´t sleep
He/ she/ it sleeps	He/ she/ it does not/ doesn´t sleep
We sleep	We do/ not/ don´t sleep
You sleep	You do/ not/ don´t sleep
They sleep	They do/ not/ don´t sleep
POSITIVO (PRESENTE CONTINUO)	NEGATIVO
I am/ I´m sleeping	I am not/ I´m not sleeping
You are/ ´re sleeping	You are/ not/aren´t sleeping
He/she/it is/´s sleeping	He/ she/it is not/ isn´t sleeping
We are/ ´re sleeping	We are/ not/aren´t sleeping
You are/ ´re sleeping	You are/ not/aren´t sleeping
They are/ ´re sleeping	They are/ not/aren´t sleeping

INTERROGATIVO (PRESENTE SIMPLE)
Do I / not/ don´t I sleep?
Do you/ not/ don´t you sleep?
Does he/ she/it / sleep/not sleep/ doesn´t he/ she/ it sleep?
Do we/ not/ don´t we sleep?
Do you/ not/ don´t you sleep?
Do they/ not/ don´t they sleep?
INTERROGATIVO (PRESENTE CONTINUO)
Am I/ not/ aren´t I sleeping?
Are you/ not/ aren´t you sleeping?
Is/he/she/it/ not/ isn´t he/ she/ it sleeping?
Are we/ not/ aren´t we sleeping?
Are you/ not/ aren´t you sleeping?
Are they/ not/ aren´t they sleeping?

2. To cost- costar

POSITIVO (PRESENTE SIMPLE)	NEGATIVO
I cost	I do/ not/ don´t cost
You cost	You do/ not/ don´t cost
He/ she/it costs	He/ she/ it does not/ doesn´t cost
We cost	We do/ not/ don´t cost
You cost	You do/ not/ don´t cost
They cost	They do/ not/ don´t cost
POSITIVO (PRESENTE CONTINUO)	NEGATIVO
I am/ I´m costing	I am/´m/ not costing
You are/ ´re costing	You are/ not/aren´t costing
He/she/it is/´s costing	He/ she/it is not/ isn´t costing
We are/ ´re costing	We are/ not/aren´t costing
You are/ ´re costing	You are/ not/aren´t costing
They are/ ´re costing	They are/ not/aren´t costing

INTERROGATIVO (PRESENTE SIMPLE)
Do I / not/ don´t I cost?
Do you/ not/ don´t you cost?
Does he/ she/it / cost /not cost / doesn´t he/ she/ it cost?
Do we/ not/ don´t we cost?
Do you/ not/ don´t you cost?
Do they/ not/ don´t they cost?
INTERROGATIVO (PRESENTE CONTINUO)
Am I/ not/ aren´t I costing?
Are you/ not/ aren´t you costing
Is/he/she/it/ not/ isn´t he/ she/ it costing?
Are we/ not/ aren´t we costing
Are you/ not/ aren´t you costing
Are they/ not/ aren´t they costing

3. To find - encontrar

POSITIVO (PRESENTE SIMPLE)	NEGATIVO
I find	I do/ not/ don´t find
You find	You do/ not/ don´t find
He/ she/ it finds	He/ she/ it does not/ doesn´t find
We find	We do/ not/ don´t find
You find	You do/ not/ don´t find
They find	They do/ not/ don´t find
POSITIVO (PRESENTE CONTINUO)	NEGATIVO
I am/ I´m finding	I am/´m/ not finding
You are/ ´re finding	You are/ not/aren´t finding
He/she/it is/´s finding	He/ she/it is not/ isn´t finding
We are/ ´re finding	We are/ not/aren´t finding
You are/ ´re finding	You are/ not/aren´t finding
They are/ ´re finding	They are/ not/aren´t finding

INTERROGATIVO (PRESENTE SIMPLE)
Do I / not/ don´t I find?
Do you/ not/ don´t you find?
Does he/ she/it / find/not find / doesn´t he/ she/ it find?
Do we/ not/ don´t we find?
Do you/ not/ don´t you find?
Do they/ not/ don´t they find?
INTERROGATIVO (PRESENTE CONTINUO)
Am I/ not/ aren´t I finding?
Are you/ not/ aren´t you finding?
Is/he/she/it/ not/ isn´t he/ she/ it finding?
Are we/ not/ aren´t we finding?
Are you/ not/ aren´t you finding?
Are they/ not/ aren´t they finding?

4. To be able, "can" - poder

POSITIVO (PRESENTE SIMPLE)	NEGATIVO
I can	I cannot/ can´t
You can	You cannot/ can´t
He/she/it can	He/ she/ it cannot/ can´t
We can	We cannot/ can´t
You can	You cannot/ can´t
They can	He/ she/it cannot/ can´t
POSITIVO (PRESENTE CONTINUO)	NEGATIVO
N/A	N/A
N/A	N/A
N/A	N/A
N/A	N/A
N/A	N/A
N/A	N/A

INTERROGATIVO (PRESENTE SIMPLE)
Can I? / Can I not?/ Can´t I?
Can you? / Can you not?/ Can´t you?
Can he/ she/ it? / Can he/ she/ it not?/ Can´t he/ she/ it?
Can we? / Can we not?/ Can´t we?
Can you? / Can you not?/ Can´t you?
Can they? / Can they not?/ Can´t they?
INTERROGATIVO (PRESENTE CONTINUO)
N/A
N/A
N/A
N/A
N/A
N/A

5. To return - Volver/ regresar

POSITIVO (PRESENTE SIMPLE)	NEGATIVO
I return	I do/ not/ don´t return
You return	You do/ not/ don´t return
He/she/it returns	He/ she/ it does not/ doesn´t return
We return	We do/ not/ don´t return
You return	You do/ not/ don´t return
They return	They do/ not/ don´t return
POSITIVO (PRESENTE CONTINUO)	NEGATIVO
I am/ I´m returning	I am/´m/ not returning
You are/ ´re returning	You are/ not/aren´t returning
He/she/it is/´s returning	He/ she/it is not/ isn´t returning
We are/ ´re returning	We are/ not/aren´t returning
You are/ ´re returning	You are/ not/aren´t returning
We are/ ´re returning	They are/ not/aren´t returning

INTERROGATIVO (PRESENTE SIMPLE)
Do I / not/ don´t I return?
Do you/ not/ don´t you return?
Does he/ she/it / return/not return / doesn´t he/ she/ it return?
Do we/ not/ don´t we return?
Do you/ not/ don´t you return?
Do they/ not/ don´t they return?
INTERROGATIVO (PRESENTE CONTINUO)
Am I/ not/ aren´t I returning?
Are you/ not/ aren´t you returning
Is/he/she/it/ not/ isn´t he/ she/ it returning?
Are we/ not/ aren´t we returning?
Are you/ not/ aren´t you returning?
Are they/ not/ aren´t they returning?

6. To remember - recordar

POSITIVO (PRESENTE SIMPLE)	NEGATIVO
I remember	I do/ not/ don´t remember
You remember	You do/ not/ don´t remember
He/ she/ it remembers	remember
We remember	We do/ not/ don´t remember
You remember	You do/ not/ don´t remember
They remember	They do/ not/ don´t remember
POSITIVO (PRESENTE CONTINUO)	NEGATIVO
I am/ I´m remembering	I am/´m/ not remembering
You are/ you´re remembering	You are/ not/aren´t remembering
He/she/it is/´s remembering	He/ she/it is not/ isn´t remembering
We are/ ´re remembering	We are/ not/aren´t remembering
You are/ ´re remembering	You are/ not/aren´t remembering
They are/ ´re remembering	They are/ not/aren´t remembering

INTERROGATIVO (PRESENTE SIMPLE)
Do I / not/ don´t I remember?
Do you/ not/ don´t you remember?
Does he/ she/it / remember/not remember / doesn´t he/ she/ it remember?
Do we/ not/ don´t we remember?
Do you/ not/ don´t you remember?
Do they/ not/ don´t they remember?
INTERROGATIVO (PRESENTE CONTINUO)
Am I/ not/ aren´t I remembering?
Are you/ not/ aren´t you remembering?
Is/he/she/it/ not/ isn´t he/ she/ it remembering?
Are we/ not/ aren´t we remembering?
Are you/ not/ aren´t you remembering?
Are they/ not/ aren´t they remembering?

PRACTICE B: (YouTube)

1. I sleep very well in Spain.
2. Do you remember this song?
3. They return/ are/´re returning/ come back/are/ ´re coming back on Friday.
4. We do not/ don´t sleep late.
5. We can open the door.
6. She finds a lot of things in her taxi.
7. The shoes cost twenty euros.
8. He does not/ doesn´t sleep/ is not/ isn´t sleeping at night.
9. I cannot/ can´t eat shellfish.
10. Can you work for me?
11. Do they sleep/ are they sleeping on the plane?
12. When do you return/ come back/ are/´re you returning/ coming back?
13. We remember it very well.
14. How do you find/ are/ ´re you finding the course?
15. How much does the house cost?
16. The car does not/ doesn´t cost much?
17. I do not/ don´t remember anything.
18. I do not/ don´t find it difficult.
19. You do not/ don´t return/ come back/ are not/ aren´t returning/ coming back until Monday.
20. You remember everything.

PRACTICE C: (YouTube)

1. To lose- perder

POSITIVO (PRESENTE SIMPLE)	NEGATIVO
I lose	I do/ not/ don´t lose
You lose	You do/ not/ don´t lose
He/ she/ it loses	He/ she/ it does not/ doesn´t lose
We lose	We do/ not/ don´t lose
You lose	You do/ not/ don´t lose
They lose	They do/ not/ don´t lose
POSITIVO (PRESENTE CONTINUO)	NEGATIVO
I am/ I´m losing	I am/´m/ not losing
You are/ ´re losing	You are/ not/aren´t losing
He/ she/ it is/´s losing	He/ she/it is not/ isn´t losing
We are/ ´re losing	We are/ not/aren´t losing
You are/ ´re losing	You are/ not/ aren´t losing
They are/ ´re losing	They are/ not/aren´t losing

INTERROGATIVO (PRESENTE SIMPLE)
Do I / not/ don´t I lose?
Do you/ not/ don´t you lose?
Does he/ she/it / lose/not lose / doesn´t he/ she/ it lose?
Do we/ not/ don´t we lose?
Do you/ not/ don´t you lose?
Do they/ not/ don´t they lose?
INTERROGATIVO (PRESENTE CONTINUO)
Am I/ not/ aren´t I losing?
Are you/ not/ aren´t you losing?
Is/he/she/it/ not/ isn´t he/ she/ it losing?
Are we/ not/ aren´t we losing?
Are you/ not/ aren´t you losing?
Are they/ not/ aren´t they losing?

2. To start- empezar/ comenzar

POSITIVO (PRESENTE SIMPLE)	NEGATIVO
I start	I do/ not/ don´t start
You start	You do/ not/ don´t start
He/ she/ it starts	He/ she/ it does not/ doesn´t start
We start	We do/ not/ don´t start
You start	You do/ not/ don´t start
They start	They do/ not/ don´t start
POSITIVO (PRESENTE CONTINUO)	NEGATIVO
I am/ I´m starting	I am/´m/ not starting
You are/ ´re starting	You are/ not/aren´t starting
He/ she/ it is/´s starting	He/ she/it is not/ isn´t starting
We are/ ´re starting	We are/ not/aren´t starting
You are/ ´re starting	You are/ not/aren´t starting
They are/ ´re starting	They are/ not/aren´t starting

INTERROGATIVO (PRESENTE SIMPLE)
Do I / not/ don´t I start?
Do you/ not/ don´t you start?
Does he/ she/it / start/not start / doesn´t he/ she/ it start?
Do we/ not/ don´t we start?
Do you/ not/ don´t you start?
Do they/ not/ don´t they start?
INTERROGATIVO (PRESENTE CONTINUO)
Am I/ not/ aren´t I starting?
Are you/ not/ aren´t you starting?
Is/he/she/it/ not/ isn´t he/ she/ it starting?
Are we/ not/ aren´t we starting?
Are you/ not/ aren´t you starting?
Are they/ not/ aren´t they starting?

3. To understand - entender

POSITIVO (PRESENTE SIMPLE)	NEGATIVO
I understand	I do/ not/ don´t understand
You understand	You do/ not/ don´t understand
He/ she/ it understands	He/ she/ it does not/ doesn´t understand
We understand	We do/ not/ don´t understand
You understand	You do/ not/ don´t understand
They understand	They do/ not/ don´t understand
POSITIVO (PRESENTE CONTINUO)	NEGATIVO
I am/ I´m understanding	I am/´m/ not understanding
You are/ ´re understanding	You are/ not/aren´t understanding
He/ she/ it is/´s understanding	He/ she/it is not/ isn´t understanding
We are/ ´re understanding	We are/ not/aren´t understanding
You are/ ´re understanding	You are/ not/aren´t understanding
They are/ ´re understanding	They are/ not/aren´t understanding

INTERROGATIVO (PRESENTE SIMPLE)
Do I / not/ don´t I understand?
Do you/ not/ don´t you understand
Does he/ she/it / understand /not understand / doesn´t he/ she/ it understand?
Do we/ not/ don´t we understand?
Do you/ not/ don´t you understand?
Do they/ not/ don´t they understand?
INTERROGATIVO (PRESENTE CONTINUO)
Am I/ not/ aren´t I understanding?
Are you/ not/ aren´t you understanding
Is/he/she/it/ not/ isn´t he/ she/ it understanding?
Are we/ not/ aren´t we understanding?
Are you/ not/ aren´t you understanding?
Are they/ not/ aren´t they understanding?

4. To prefer - preferir

POSITIVO (PRESENTE SIMPLE)	NEGATIVO
I prefer	I do/ not/ don´t prefer
You prefer	You do/ not/ don´t prefer
He/ she/it prefers	He/ she/ it does not/ doesn´t prefer
We prefer	We do/ not/ don´t prefer
You prefer	You do/ not/ don´t prefer
They prefer	They do/ not/ don´t prefer
POSITIVO (PRESENTE CONTINUO)	NEGATIVO
N/A	N/A
N/A	N/A
N/A	N/A
N/A	N/A
N/A	N/A
N/A	N/A

INTERROGATIVO (PRESENTE SIMPLE)
Do I / not/ don´t I prefer?
Do you/ not/ don´t you prefer?
Does he/ she/it / prefer/not prefer / doesn´t he/ she/ it prefer?
Do we/ not/ don´t we prefer?
Do you/ not/ don´t you prefer?
Do they/ not/ don´t they prefer?
INTERROGATIVO (PRESENTE CONTINUO)
N/A
N/A
N/A
N/A
N/A
N/A

5. To think- pensar

POSITIVO (PRESENTE SIMPLE)	NEGATIVO
I think	I do/ not/ don´t think
You think	You do/ not/ don´t think
He/ she/ it thinks	He/ she/ it does not/ doesn´t think
We think	We do/ not/ don´t think
You think	You do/ not/ don´t think
They think	They do/ not/ don´t think
POSITIVO (PRESENTE CONTINUO)	NEGATIVO
I am/ I´m thinking	I am/´m/ not thinking
You are/ ´re thinking	You are/ not/aren´t thinking
He/ she/ it is/´s thinking	He/ she/it is not/ isn´t thinking
We are/ ´re thinking	We are/ not/aren´t thinking
You are/ ´re thinking	You are/ not/aren´t thinking
They are/ ´re thinking	They are/ not/aren´t thinking

INTERROGATIVO (PRESENTE SIMPLE)
Do I / not/ don´t I think?
Do you/ not/ don´t you think
Does he/ she/it / want/not want / doesn´t he/ she/ it think?
Do we/ not/ don´t we think?
Do you/ not/ don´t you think?
Do they/ not/ don´t they think?
INTERROGATIVO (PRESENTE CONTINUO)
Am I/ not/ aren´t I thinking?
Are you/ not/ aren´t you thinking
Is/ he/she/it/ not/ isn´t he/ she/ it thinking?
Are we/ not/ aren´t we thinking?
Are you/ not/ aren´t you thinking?
Are they/ not/ aren´t they thinking?

6. To want - querer

POSITIVO (PRESENTE SIMPLE)	NEGATIVO
I want	I do/ not/ don´t want
You want	You do/ not/ don´t want
He/ she/ it wants	He/ she/ it does not/ doesn´t want
We want	We do/ not/ don´t want
You want	You do/ not/ don´t want
They want	They do/ not/ don´t want
POSITIVO (PRESENTE CONTINUO)	NEGATIVO
N/A	N/A
N/A	N/A
N/A	N/A
N/A	N/A
N/A	N/A
N/A	N/A

INTERROGATIVO (PRESENTE SIMPLE)
Do I / not/ don´t I want?
Do you / not/ don´t you want?
Does he/ she/it / want/not want / doesn´t he/ she/ it want?
Do we / not/ don´t we want?
Do you / not/ don´t you want?
Do they / not/ don´t they want?
INTERROGATIVO (PRESENTE CONTINUO)
N/A
N/A
N/A
N/A
N/A
N/A

PRACTICE D: (YouTube)

1. The film starts/ is/´s/starting at nine o´clock.
2. Do you understand verbs in English?
3. He prefers red wine.
4. What do you/ are/´re you thinking about?
5. The match does not/ doesn´t start/ is not/isn´t starting until six in the evening.
6. We always lose/ we are/´re always losing our sunglasses.
7. They want a house in England.
8. I do not/ don´t want to learn German, I want to learn English.
9. Which car do you prefer?
10. What time does the class start?
11. I do not/ don´t understand bad people.
12. We understand everything.
13. Do not/ don´t think badly.
14. What things do you lose in the house?
15. Which language do you want to learn?
16. You think that Spain is very pretty.
17. She understands Chines very well.
18. He wants paella for lunch.
19. We do not/ don´t want to speak/ talk to you.
20. I want to have paella.

DIPTHONGS 3-

PRACTICE E: (YouTube)

1. To get- conseguir

POSITIVO (PRESENTE SIMPLE)	NEGATIVO
I get	I do/ not/ don´t get
You get	You do/ not/ don´t get
He/ she/it gets	He/ she/ it does not/ doesn´t get
We get	We do/ not/ don´t get
You get	You do/ not/ don´t get
They get	They do/ not/ don´t get
POSITIVO (PRESENTE CONTINUO)	NEGATIVO
I am/ I´m getting	I am/´m/ not getting
You are/ ´re getting	You are/ not/aren´t getting
He/ she/ it is/´s getting	He/ she/it is not/ isn´t getting
We are/ ´re getting	We are/ not/aren´t getting
You are/ ´re getting	You are/ not/aren´t getting
They are/ ´re getting	They are/ not/aren´t getting

INTERROGATIVO (PRESENTE SIMPLE)
Do I / not/ don´t I get?
Do you / not/ don´t you get?
Does he/ she/it not/ doesn´t he/ she/ it get?
Do we / not/ don´t we get?
Do you / not/ don´t you get?
Do they / not/ don´t they get?
INTERROGATIVO (PRESENTE CONTINUO)
Am I/ not/ aren´t I getting?
Are you/ not/ aren´t you getting?
Is/he/she/it/ not/ isn´t he/ she/ it getting?
Are we/ not/ aren´t we getting?
Are you/ not/ aren´t you getting?
Are they/ not/ aren´t they getting?

2. To fry - freir

POSITIVO (PRESENTE SIMPLE)	NEGATIVO
I fry	I do/ not/ don´t fry
You fry	You do/ not/ don´t fry
He/ she/ it fries	He/ she/ it does not/ doesn´t fry
We fry	We do/ not/ don´t fry
You fry	You do/ not/ don´t fry
They fry	They do/ not/ don´t fry
POSITIVO (PRESENTE CONTINUO)	NEGATIVO
I am/ I´m frying	I am/´m/ not frying
You are/ ´re frying	You are/ not/aren´t frying
He/ she/ it is/´s frying	He/ she/it is not/ isn´t frying
We are/ ´re frying	We are/ not/aren´t frying
You are/ ´re frying	You are/ not/aren´t frying
They are/ ´re frying	They are/ not/aren´t frying

INTERROGATIVO (PRESENTE SIMPLE)
Do I / not/ don´t I fry?
Do you / not/ don´t you fry?
Does he/ she/it not/ doesn´t he/ she/ it fry?
Do we / not/ don´t we fry?
Do you / not/ don´t you fry?
Do they / not/ don´t they fry?
INTERROGATIVO (PRESENTE CONTINUO)
Am I/ not/ aren´t I frying?
Are you/ not/ aren´t you frying?
Is/he/she/it/ not/ isn´t he/ she/ it frying?
Are we/ not/ aren´t we frying?
Are you/ not/ aren´t you frying?
Are they/ not/ aren´t they frying?

3. To ask for/ order/ request- pedir

POSITIVO (PRESENTE SIMPLE)	NEGATIVO
I ask for	I do/ not/ don´t ask for
You ask for	You do/ not/ don´t ask for
He/ she/it asks for	He/ she/ it does not/ doesn´t ask for
We ask for	We do/ not/ don´t ask for
You ask for	You do/ not/ don´t ask for
They ask for	They do/ not/ don´t ask for
POSITIVO (PRESENTE CONTINUO)	NEGATIVO
I am/ I´m asking for	I am/´m/ not asking for
You are/ ´re asking for	You are/ not/aren´t asking for
He/ she/ it is/´s asking for	He/ she/it is not/ isn´t asking for
We are/ ´re asking for	We are/ not/aren´t asking for
You are/ ´re asking for	You are/ not/aren´t asking for
They are/ ´re asking for	They are/ not/aren´t asking for

INTERROGATIVO (PRESENTE SIMPLE)
Do I / not/ don´t I ask for?
Do you / not/ don´t you ask for?
Does he/ she/it not/ doesn´t he/ she/ it ask for?
Do we/ not/ don´t we ask for?
Do you / not/ don´t you ask for?
Do they / not/ don´t they ask for?
INTERROGATIVO (PRESENTE CONTINUO)
Am I/ not/ aren´t I asking for?
Are you/ not/ aren´t you asking for?
Is/he/she/it/ not/ isn´t he/ she/ it asking for?
Are we/ not/ aren´t we asking for?
Are you/ not/ aren´t you asking for?
Are they/ not/ aren´t they asking for?

4. To serve- servir

POSITIVO (PRESENTE SIMPLE)	NEGATIVO
I serve	I do/ not/ don´t serve
You serve	You do/ not/ don´t serve
He/ she/ it serves	He/ she/ it does not/ doesn´t serve
We serve	We do/ not/ don´t serve
You serve	You do/ not/ don´t serve
They serve	They do/ not/ don´t serve
POSITIVO (PRESENTE CONTINUO)	NEGATIVO
I am/ I´m serving	I am/´m/ not serving
You are/ ´re serving	You are/ not/aren´t serving
He/ she/ it is/´s serving	He/ she/it is not/ isn´t serving
We are/ ´re serving	We are/ not/aren´t serving
You are/ ´re serving	You are/ not/aren´t serving
They are/ ´re serving	They are/ not/aren´t serving

INTERROGATIVO (PRESENTE SIMPLE)
Do I / not/ don´t I serve?
Do you / not/ don´t you serve?
Does he/ she/it not/ doesn´t he/ she/ it serve?
Do we / not/ don´t you serve?
Do you / not/ don´t you serve?
Do they / not/ don´t you serve?
INTERROGATIVO (PRESENTE CONTINUO)
Am I/ not/ aren´t I serving?
Are you/ not/ aren´t you serving?
Is/he/she/it/ not/ isn´t he/ she/ it serving?
Are we/ not/ aren´t we serving?
Are you/ not/ aren´t you serving?
Are they/ not/ aren´t they serving?

5. To measure- medir

POSITIVO (PRESENTE SIMPLE)	NEGATIVO
I measure	I do/ not/ don´t measure
You measure	You do/ not/ don´t measure
He/ she/it measures	He/ she/ it does not/ doesn´t measure
We measure	We do/ not/ don´t measure
You measure	You do/ not/ don´t measure
They measure	They do/ not/ don´t measure
POSITIVO (PRESENTE CONTINUO)	NEGATIVO
I am/ I´m measuring	I am/´m/ not measuring
You are/ ´re measuring	You are/ not/aren´t measuring
He/ she/ it is/´s measuring	He/ she/it is not/ isn´t measuring
We are/ ´re measuring	We are/ not/aren´t measuring
You are/ ´re measuring	You are/ not/aren´t measuring
They are/ ´re measuring	They are/ not/aren´t measuring

INTERROGATIVO (PRESENTE SIMPLE)
Do I / not/ don´t I measure?
Do you / not/ don´t you measure?
Does he/ she/it not/ doesn´t he/ she/ it measure?
Do we / not/ don´t we measure?
Do you / not/ don´t you measure?
Do they / not/ don´t they measure?
INTERROGATIVO (PRESENTE CONTINUO)
Am I/ not/ aren´t I measuring?
Are you/ not/ aren´t you measuring?
Is/he/she/it/ not/ isn´t he/ she/ it measuring?
Are we/ not/ aren´t we measuring?
Are you/ not/ aren´t you measuring?
Are they/ not/ aren´t they measuring?

6. To follow - seguir

POSITIVO (PRESENTE SIMPLE)	NEGATIVO
I follow	I do/ not/ don´t follow
You follow	You do/ not/ don´t follow
He/ she/ it follows	He/ she/ it does not/ doesn´t follow
We follow	we do/ not/ don´t follow
You follow	You do/ not/ don´t follow
They follow	They do/ not/ don´t follow
POSITIVO (PRESENTE CONTINUO)	NEGATIVO
I am/ I´m following	I am/´m/ not following
You are/ ´re following	You are/ not/aren´t following
He/ she/ it is/´s following	He/ she/it is not/ isn´t following
We are/ ´re following	We are/ not/aren´t following
You are/ ´re following	You are/ not/aren´t following
They are/ ´re following	They are/ not/aren´t following

INTERROGATIVO (PRESENTE SIMPLE)
Do I / not/ don´t I follow?
Do you / not/ don´t you follow?
Does he/ she/it not/ doesn´t he/ she/ it follow?
Do we / not/ don´t we follow?
Do you / not/ don´t you follow?
Do they / not/ don´t they follow?
INTERROGATIVO (PRESENTE CONTINUO)
Am I/ not/ aren´t I following?
Are you/ not/ aren´t you following?
Is/he/she/it/ not/ isn´t he/ she/ it following?
Are we/ not/ aren´t we following?
Are you/ not/ aren´t you following?
Are they/ not/ aren´t they following?

PRACTICE F: (YouTube)

1. I do not/ don´t fry a lot of food.
2. What do you order to drink with a paella?
3. She never serves wine with dinner.
4. How can you get a good job?

5. We measure/ are/ ´re measuring the curtains.
6. Do you follow/ are you following me?
7. He does not/ doesn´t/ is not/ isn´t following the course very well.
8. I do not/ don´t ask/ am not asking for anything from you.
9. What do they serve/ are they serving for breakfast?
10. She fries a hamburger every Saturday.
11. What do you measure/ are/ ´re you measuring?
12. Now is a good time to get a kiss.
13. Do you fry/ are you frying eggs with breakfast?
14. I do not/ don´t measure/ am not measuring the water I drink.
15. The waiter serves/ is/ ´s serving the drinks on the terrace.
16. They always order a beer in the bar.
17. We get/ are getting a job.
18. You follow/ are/ ´re following the yellow car.
19. Why do you ask/ are/ ´re you asking for so much?
20. We do not/ don´t fry/ are not/ aren´t frying anything.

CONVERSATION PRACTICE DIPTHONGS- PRACTICE G: (YouTube) - FREE ANSWERS

1. What do you normally order in a Chinese restaurant?
2. What time do you start work?
3. Do you sleep well in other people´s houses?
4. How much does a bottle of milk cost in Spain?
5. How do you find a good mechanic in Spain?
6. What time do you start to watch the television?
7. Do you understand much French?
8. Do you lose many things in the house?
9. Do you prefer red, white or rosé wine?
10. Who do you remember more from school?
11. Do you return often to your town?
12. Can you see the sea from your house?
13. Do you think England is better than your country?
14. Why do you want to speak Spanish?
15. How do you get a good job in Spain?
16. What do they normally serve for breakfast in a Spanish restaurant?
17. Do you fry a lot of food?
18. Do you follow/ are you following this course?
19. Does it cost a lot to eat in a restaurant in your area?
20. Do you prefer to have a coffee at home or in a bar?

21. Do you count the calories do you have every day?
22. Do you understand why it is important to learn English?

24. DIPTHONGS - PRACTICE IN CONTEXT

PRACTICE A:

	VERB	INFINITIVE	ENGLISH	PERSON
1	es	ser	to be	3rd person singular
2	vive	vivir	To live	3rd person singular
3	No recuerdo	recordar	To remember	1st person singular
4	recuerdo	recordar	To remember	1st person singular
5	está	estar	To be	3rd person singular
6	va	ir	To go	3rd person singular
7	pide	pedir	To order	3rd person singular
8	sirve	servir	To serve	3rd person singular
9	vuelve	volver	To return	3rd person singular
10	comer	comer	To have lunch	"Ing"/infinitive
11	llega	llegar	To arrive	3rd person singular
12	piensan	pensar	To think	3rd person plural
13	cuentan	contar	To count	3rd person plural
14	tienen	tener	To have	3rd person plural
15	comprar	comprar	To buy	infinitive
16	quieren	querer	To want	3rd person singular
17	cuesta	costar	To cost	3rd person singular
18	tienen	tener	To have	3rd person plural
19	necesitan	necesitar	To need	3rd person plural
20	duermen	dormir	To sleep	3rd person plural
21	piensan	pensar	To think	3rd person plural
22	pueden	poder	can	Verbo modal
23	conseguir	conseguir	To get	Infinitive
24	comprar	comprar	To buy	Infinitive
25	cenar	cenar	To have dinner	"ing"/infinitve
26	Lava/ friega	lavar	To was	3rd person singular
27	comienza	comenzar	To start	3rd person singular
28	leer	leer	To read	Infinitive

29	comprenden	comprender	To understand	3rd person plural
30	conseguir	conseguir	To get	Infinitive
31	pueden	poder	can	Verbo modal
32	salir	salir	To go out	Infinitive

PRACTICE B: (YouTube)

Pedro Martínez is a mechanic and he lives in Alicante. I do not/ don´t remember exactly where, but I remember that his house is near the beach. Every Friday, he goes to the bar and he orders a menu of the day that the waiter serves on the terrace.

He returns to his house after having lunch at 5, and at 8 his girlfriend Carmen arrives. They think about their future and they count the money they have to buy a house. The house that they want costs 130 thousand euros, they have 100 thousand and they need more. They do not/ don´t sleep at night because they think about how they can get enough money to buy the house.

After having dinner, Pedro washes the dishes and Carmen starts to read the newspaper. They both understand that to get the money for the house, they can not/ can´t go out in the evenings.

PRACTICE C: (YouTube)

1. What does Pedro do? He is/´s a mechanic.
2. Where does he live? He lives in Alicante.
3. Do I remember exactly where his house is? No, but I remember that it is/´s near the beach.
4. Where does he go every Friday? He goes to the bar.
5. What does he order? He orders a menu of the day.
6. Where does the waiter serve the food? The waiter serves the food on the terrace.
7. What time does he return to his house? He returns to his house at five.
8. What time does his girlfriend, Carmen, arrive? Carmen arrives at eight.
9. What do they think about? They think about their future.
10. What do they count? They count the money they have to buy the house.
11. How much does the house they want cost? The house that they want costs 130 thousand euros.
12. How much do they have? They have 100 thousand.
13. Why can they not/ can´t they sleep at night? They can´t sleep at night because they think about how they can get enough money to buy the house.

14. What does Pedro do after having dinner? He washes the dishes.
15. What does Carmen do? Carmen starts to read the paper.
16. What do they both understand? They both understand that to get the money for the house they can not/ can´t go out in the evening.

24. THE VERB "TENER" – TO HAVE/ HAVE GOT

PRACTICE A: FREE ANSWERS

PRACTICE B: (YouTube)

1. I have/have got ten euros.
2. Do you have/ Have you got my books?
3. She has/ has got a new car.
4. Does he have/ Has he got the cups?
5. We don´t have/ havn´t got a house.
6. You have/ have got a lot of friends.
7. They have/ have got five cousins.
8. I have/ have got the money.
9. I do not/ don´t have/ have not/ haven´t got a cat.
10. Who has/ has got the keys?
11. Why does she not have/ hasn´t she got time?
12. They do not/ don´t have/ have not/ haven´t got a garden.
13. You do not/ don´t have/ haven´t got a big car.
14. Do you have/ have you got a question?
15. Who has/ has got the answer?
16. Do we have/ have we got anything in the fridge?
17. I do not/ don´t/ have not got/ haven´t got much time.
18. He does not/ doesn´t have/ hasn´t got brothers and sisters.
19. What wine do you have/ have you got?
20. I have/ have got two dogs.

PRACTICE C: (YouTube)

1. You are thirty (years old).
2. Mary is forty-five (years old).
3. My car is ten years old.
4. How old is your brother?
5. These boys are fifteen (years old).

6. His/her/their cat is eight (years old).
7. How old are they?
8. The town/ village is two hundred years old.
9. You are younger than me.
10. He is older than her.

PRACTICE D: (YouTube)

1. Because I am hungry.
2. Because he is thirsty.
3. Because they are tired.
4. Because I am cold.
5. Because you are lucky.
6. Because you are right.
7. Because I am in a hurry.
8. Because they are scared.
9. Because she is not right.
10. Because I am hot.

PRACTICE E: (YouTube)

1. Do I have to/ have I got to read this book?
2. You have to/ have got to watch this film.
3. We have to/ have got to wash the car every Saturday.
4. She has to/ has got to open the window every morning.
5. We have to/ have got to decide now.
6. You have to/ have got to sell your car.
7. They do not/ don´t have to/ have not/n´t got to eat their breakfast.
8. You have to/ have got to take the dog to the park.
9. We have to/ have got to buy wine for the party.
10. You do not/ don´t have to/ have not/n´t got to wait here.

26. "GO-GO" VERBS

PRACTICE A: (YouTube)

1. To come- venir

POSITIVO (PRESENTE SIMPLE)	NEGATIVO
I come	I do not/ don´t come
You come	You do not/ don´t come
He/ she/ it comes	He/ she/it does not/ doesn´t come
We come	We do not/ don´t come
You come	You do not/ don´t come
They come	They do not/ don´t come
POSITIVO (PRESENTE CONTINUO)	NEGATIVO
I am / I´m coming	I am not/ I´m not coming
You are/ ´re coming	You are not/´re not/ aren´t coming
He/ she/ it is/´s coming	He/she/it is not/ isn´t coming
We are/ ´re coming	We are not/´re not/ aren´t coming
You are/ ´re coming	You are not/´re not/ aren´t coming
They are/ ´re coming	They are not/´re not/ aren´t coming

INTERROGATIVO (PRESENTE SIMPLE)
Do I/ not/ don´t I come?
Do you/ not/ don´t you come?
Does he/ she/ it/ not/ doesn´t he/ she/ it come?
Do we/ not/ don´t we come?
Do you/ not/ don´t you come?
Do they/ not/ don´t they come?
INTERROGATIVO (PRESENTE CONTINUO)
Am I/ not/ aren´t I coming?
Are you/ not/ aren´t you coming?
Is he/ she/ it not/ isn´t he/ she/ it coming?
Are we/ not/ aren´t we coming?
Are you/ not/ aren´t you coming?
Are they/ not/ aren´t they coming?

2. To say – decir

POSITIVO (PRESENTE SIMPLE)	NEGATIVO
I say	I do not/ don´t say
You say	You do not/ don´t say
He/ she/ it says	He/ she/it does not/ doesn´t say
We say	We do not/ don´t say
You say	You do not/ don´t say
They say	They do not/ don´t say
POSITIVO (PRESENTE CONTINUO)	NEGATIVO
I am / I´m saying	I am not/ I´m not saying
You are/ ´re saying	You are not/´re not/ aren´t saying
He/ she/ it is/´s saying	He/she/it is not/ isn´t saying
We are/ ´re saying	We are not/´re not/ aren´t saying
You are/ ´re saying	You are not/´re not/ aren´t saying
They are/ ´re saying	They are not/´re not/ aren´t saying

INTERROGATIVO (PRESENTE SIMPLE)
Do I/ not/ don´t I say?
Do you/ not/ don´t you say?
Does he/ she/ it/ not/ doesn´t he/ she/ it say?
Do we/ not/ don´t we say?
Do you/ not/ don´t you say?
Do they/ not/ don´t they say?
INTERROGATIVO (PRESENTE CONTINUO)
Am I/ not/ aren´t I saying?
Are you/ not/ aren´t you saying
Is he/ she/ it not/ isn´t he/ she/ it saying?
Are we/ not/ aren´t we saying?
Are you/ not/ aren´t you saying?
Are they/ not/ aren´t they saying?

3. To tell- contar

POSITIVO (PRESENTE SIMPLE)	NEGATIVO
I tell	I do not/ don't tell
You tell	You do not/ don't tell
He/ she/ it tells	He/ she/it does not/ doesn't tell
We tell	We do not/ don't tell
You tell	You do not/ don't tell
They tell	They do not/ don't tell
POSITIVO (PRESENTE CONTINUO)	NEGATIVO
I am / I'm telling	I am not/ I'm not telling
You are/ 're telling	You are not/'re not/ aren't telling
He/ she/ it is/'s telling	He/she/it is not/ isn't telling
We are/ 're telling	We are not/'re not/ aren't telling
You are/ 're telling	You are not/'re not/ aren't telling
They are/ 're telling	They are not/'re not/ aren't telling

INTERROGATIVO (PRESENTE SIMPLE)
Do I/ not/ don't I tell
Do you/ not/ don't you tell?
Does he/ she/ it/ not/ doesn't he/ she/ it tell?
Do we/ not/ don't we tell?
Do you/ not/ don't you tell?
Do they/ not/ don't they tell?
INTERROGATIVO (PRESENTE CONTINUO)
Am I/ not/ aren't I telling?
Are you/ not/ aren't you telling?
Is he/ she/ it not/ isn't he/ she/ it telling?
Are we/ not/ aren't we telling?
Are you/ not/ aren't you telling
Are they/ not/ aren't they telling?

4. To do- hacer

POSITIVO (PRESENTE SIMPLE)	NEGATIVO
I do	I do not/ don´t do
You do	You do not/ don´t do
He/ she it does	He/ she/it does not/ doesn´t do
We do	We do not/ don´t do
You do	You do not/ don´t do
They do	They do not/ don´t do
POSITIVO (PRESENTE CONTINUO)	NEGATIVO
I am / I´m doing	I am not/ I´m not doing
You are/ ´re doing	You are not/´re not/ aren´t doing
He/ she/ it is/´s doing	He/she/it is not/ isn´t doing
We are/ ´re doing	We are not/´re not/ aren´t doing
You are/ ´re doing	You are not/´re not/ aren´t doing
They are/ ´re doing	They are not/´re not/ aren´t doing

INTERROGATIVO (PRESENTE SIMPLE)
Do I/ not/ don´t I do?
Do you/ not/ don´t you do?
Does he/ she/ it/ not/ doesn´t he/ she/ it do?
Do we/ not/ don´t we do?
Do you/ not/ don´t you do?
Do they/ not/ don´t they do?
INTERROGATIVO (PRESENTE CONTINUO)
Am I/ not/ aren´t I doing?
Are you/ not/ aren´t you doing?
Is he/ she/ it not/ isn´t he/ she/ it doing?
Are we/ not/ aren´t we doing?
Are you/ not/ aren´t you doing?
Are they/ not/ aren´t they doing?

5. to make- hacer

POSITIVO (PRESENTE SIMPLE)	NEGATIVO
I make	I do not/ don´t make
You make	You do not/ don´t make
He/ she/ it makes	He/ she/it does not/ doesn´t make
We make	We do not/ don´t make
You make	You do not/ don´t make
They make	They do not/ don´t make
POSITIVO (PRESENTE CONTINUO)	NEGATIVO
I am / I´m making	I am not/ I´m not making
You are/ ´re making	You are not/´re not/ aren´t making
He/ she/ it is/´s making	He/she/it is not/ isn´t making
We are/ ´re making	We are not/´re not/ aren´t making
You are/ ´re making	You are not/´re not/ aren´t making
They are/ ´re making	They are not/´re not/ aren´t making

INTERROGATIVO (PRESENTE SIMPLE)
Do I/ not/ don´t I make?
Do you/ not/ don´t you make?
Does he/ she/ it/ not/ doesn´t he/ she/ it make?
Do we/ not/ don´t we make?
Do you/ not/ don´t you make?
Do they/ not/ don´t they make?
INTERROGATIVO (PRESENTE CONTINUO)
Am I/ not/ aren´t I making?
Are you/ not/ aren´t you making?
Is he/ she/ it not/ isn´t he/ she/ it making?
Are we/ not/ aren´t we making?
Are you/ not/ aren´t you making?
Are they/ not/ aren´t they making?

6. to hear- oir

POSITIVO (PRESENTE SIMPLE)	NEGATIVO
I hear	I do not/ don´t hear
You hear	You do not/ don´t hear
He/ she/ it hears	He/ she/it does not/ doesn´t hear
We hear	We do not/ don´t hear
You hear	You do not/ don´t hear
They hear	They do not/ don´t hear
POSITIVO (PRESENTE CONTINUO)	NEGATIVO
I am / I´m hearing	I am not/ I´m not hearing
You are/ ´re hearing	You are not/´re not/ aren´t hearing
He/ she/ it is/´s hearing	He/she/it is not/ isn´t hearing
We are/ ´re hearing	We are not/´re not/ aren´t hearing
You are/ ´re hearing	You are not/´re not/ aren´t hearing
They are/ ´re hearing	They are not/´re not/ aren´t hearing

INTERROGATIVO (PRESENTE SIMPLE)
Do I/ not/ don´t I hear?
Do you/ not/ don´t you hear?
Does he/ she/ it/ not/ doesn´t he/ she/ it hear?
Do we/ not/ don´t we hear?
Do you/ not/ don´t you hear?
Do they/ not/ don´t they hear?
INTERROGATIVO (PRESENTE CONTINUO)
Am I/ not/ aren´t I hearing?
Are you/ not/ aren´t you hearing?
Is he/ she/ it not/ isn´t he/ she/ it hearing?
Are we/ not/ aren´t we hearing?
Are you/ not/ aren´t you hearing?
Are they/ not/ aren´t they hearing?

7. to put - poner

POSITIVO (PRESENTE SIMPLE)	NEGATIVO
I put	I do not/ don´t put
You put	You do not/ don´t put
He/she/it puts	He/ she/it does not/ doesn´t put
We put	We do not/ don´t put
You put	You do not/ don´t put
They put	They do not/ don´t put
POSITIVO (PRESENTE CONTINUO)	NEGATIVO
I am / I´m putting	I am not/ I´m not putting
You are/ ´re putting	You are not/´re not/ aren´t putting
He/ she/ it is/´s putting	He/she/it is not/ isn´t putting
We are/ ´re putting	We are not/´re not/ aren´t putting
You are/ ´re putting	You are not/´re not/ aren´t putting
They are/ ´re putting	They are not/´re not/ aren´t putting

INTERROGATIVO (PRESENTE SIMPLE)
Do I/ not/ don´t I put?
Do you/ not/ don´t you put?
Does he/ she/ it/ not/ doesn´t he/ she/ it put?
Do we/ not/ don´t we put?
Do you/ not/ don´t you put?
Do they/ not/ don´t they put?
INTERROGATIVO (PRESENTE CONTINUO)
Am I/ not/ aren´t I putting?
Are you/ not/ aren´t you putting?
Is he/ she/ it not/ isn´t he/ she/ it putting?
Are we/ not/ aren´t we putting?
Are you/ not/ aren´t you putting?
Are they/ not/ aren´t they putting?

8. To bring- traer

POSITIVO (PRESENTE SIMPLE)	NEGATIVO
I bring	I do not/ don´t bring
You bring	You do not/ don´t bring
He/ she/ it brings	He/ she/it does not/ doesn´t bring
We bring	We do not/ don´t bring
You bring	You do not/ don´t bring
They bring	They do not/ don´t bring
POSITIVO (PRESENTE CONTINUO)	NEGATIVO
I am / I´m bringing	I am not/ I´m not bringing
You are/ ´re bringing	You are not/´re not/ aren´t bringing
He/ she/ it is/´s bringing	He/she/it is not/ isn´t bringing
We are/ ´re bringing	We are not/´re not/ aren´t bringing
You are/ ´re bringing	You are not/´re not/ aren´t bringing
They are/ ´re bringing	They are not/´re not/ aren´t bringing

INTERROGATIVO (PRESENTE SIMPLE)
Do I/ not/ don´t I bring?
Do you/ not/ don´t you bring?
Does he/ she/ it/ not/ doesn´t he/ she/ it bring?
Do we/ not/ don´t we bring?
Do you/ not/ don´t you bring?
Do they/ not/ don´t they bring?
INTERROGATIVO (PRESENTE CONTINUO)
Am I/ not/ aren´t I bringing?
Are you/ not/ aren´t you bringing?
Is he/ she/ it not/ isn´t he/ she/ it bringing?
Are we/ not/ aren´t we bringing?
Are you/ not/ aren´t you bringing?
Are they/ not/ aren´t they bringing?

PRACTICE B: (YouTube) (free answers)

1. Do you go out much?
2. How many brothers and sisters do you have?
3. Who comes to your house on Sundays?

4. What do you hear outside your house in the morning?
5. What do you say to an English person on their birthday?
6. What do you normally put on your bedside table?
7. What do you normally make for lunch on Sunday?
8. Do you have a dog?
9. What do you say when you are angry?
10. Do you come to Spain often?
11. Do you hear much English where you live?
12. Where do you put your keys in the house?
13. When do you make a paella?
14. What do you bring with you to Spanish class?

27. TO LIKE- "GUSTAR"

PRACTICE A: (YouTube)

1. They like swimmimg.
2. Do you like chocolate?
3. We like fast cars.
4. We are not liking this at all.
5. Do you like reading?
6. He likes to swim.
7. I like to sing.
8. Does he not/ doesn´t he like studying?
9. We do not/don´t like speaking Spanish.
10. We like to go out on Saturdays.
11. She likes going out with her friends.
12. Do you like studying English?
13. They like Spanish food.
14. I like cats.
15. I do not/don´t like dogs.
16. Do you not/ don´t you like football?
17. We do not/ don´t like travelling by plane.
18. I like these shoes.
19. Are you liking this situation?
20. Do they not/ don´t they like you?
21. He doen´t like speaking Spanish.
22. She likes drinking coffee.
23. Do we not/ don´t we like wine?

24. Do you like swimming in the sea?
25. Are they liking being in London?

28. TO LIKE/ LOVE- GUSTAR/ENCANTAR

PRACTICA A: (FREE ANSWERS) (YOUTUBE)

1. Do you like dancing?
2. Do you like animals?
3. Do you like eating meat?
4. Do you like drinking wine?
5. Do you like going to the cinema?
6. Do you like reading?
7. Do you like working?
8. Do you like chocolate?
9. Do you like pasta?
10. Do you like the rain?
11. Do you like England?
12. Do you like walking?
13. Do you like studying English?
14. Do you like going to the beach?
15. Do you like sunbathing?
16. Do you like cooking?
17. Do you like cleaning?
18. Do you like singing on karaoke?
19. Do you like playing golf?
20. Do you like playing sport?
21. Do you like watching the telly?
22. Do you like speaking on the phone?
23. Do you like going out with friends?
24. Do you like eating in restaurants?
25. Do you like fruit?
26. Do you like shellfish?

29. "IR" - TO GO - THE HIGHLY IRREGULAR 'IR' VERB

PRACTICE A: (YouTube)

1. Where are you going?

2. They go to the beach every week.
3. We go to the bar every Sunday.
4. Where do you go on Saturdays?
5. She goes/ is going to work on the bus.
6. I go to the hospital every Tuesday morning.
7. When I need vegetables, I go to the market.
8. My brother always goes to the football.
9. To get a permit, you(s) have to go to the Town Hall.
10. When do they go/ are they going to the cinema?
11. I go to Spain every year.
12. We go to their house on Mondays.
13. They go to his house on Tuesdays.
14. Do you go to the shops often?
15. Why do you not/ don´t you/ go/ are you not/ aren´t you go to his house?

30. AUNT KATHY/ TIA KATHY.

PRACTICE A:

VERB IN CONTEXT	INFINITIVE	ENGLISH	PERSON
1. es	ser	To be	3a p.singular
2. vive	vivir	To live	3a p.singular
3. vive	vivir	To live	3a p.singular
4. vive	vivir	To live	3a p.singular
5. tiene	tener	To have	3a p.singular
6. es	ser	To be	3a p.singular
7. es	ser	To be	3a p.singular
8. tiene	tener	To have	3a p.singular
9. es	ser	To be	3a p.singular
10. tiene	tener	To have	3a p.singular
11. está	estar	To be	3a p.singular
12. tiene	tener	To have	3a p.singular
13. es	ser	To be	3a p.singular
14. tiene	tener	To have	3a p.singular
15. termina	terminar	To finish	3a p.singular
16. llega	llegar	To arrive	3a p.singular
17. está	estar	To be	3a p.singular
18. sube	subir	To go up	3a p.singular
19. gustan	gustar	To like	3a p.singular

20. quiere	querer	To want	3a p.singular
21. hacer	hacer	To do	infinitive
22. llega	llegar	To arrive	3a p.singular
23. saca	sacar	To take out	3a p.singular
24. abre	abrir	To open	3a p.singular
25. entra	entrar	To enter	3a p.singular
26. viene	venir	To come	3a p.singular
27. decir	decir	To say	infinitive
28. hace	hacer	To make	3a p.singular
29. entra	entrar	To enter	3a p.singular
30. enciende	encender	To turn on	3a p.singular
31. entra	entrar	To enter	3a p.singular
32. hace	hacer	To make	3a p.singular
33. vuelve	volver	To return	3a p.singular
34. lee	leer	To read	3a p.singular
35. se sienta	sentarse	To sit down	3a p.singular
36. empieza	empezar	To start	3a p.singular
37. leer	leer	To read	infinitive
38. apaga	apagar	To turn off	3a p.singular
39. se va	irse	To go	3a p.singular
40. prepara	preparar	To prepare	3a p.singular
41. enciende	encender	To turn on	3a p.singular
42. llama	llamar	To call	3a p.singular
43. charlan	charlar	To chat	3a p. plural
44. lava	lavar	To wash	3a p.singular
45. decide	decidir	To decide	3a p.singular
46. acostarse	acostarse	To go to bed	infinitive

PRACTICE B:

Kathy Brown is my aunt, my mother's sister. She lives in the south of England. She lives in a small, clean and tidy flat in Reading city centre. She lives alone but has a small white cat. The cat's name is "Luna".

Kathy is tall, dark and has grey eyes. She is very attractive and is thirty-five years old. She is not/isn't married but has a boyfriend, Lewis. Aunt Kathy is a lawyer and has a big office near to her house.

She finishes work at seven o'clock in the evening and when she arrives home she is very tired. In her flat there are two bedrooms, one bathroom, a living room, a dining room, and an office.

She goes up the stairs because she doesn't like lifts and she wants to do more exercise. When she arrives at the third floor she takes out her key, opens the door and enters. Luna always comes to say hello. She makes a lot of noise for a cat.

Kathy enters the office and turns on the computer. Then she goes into the kitchen where she makes a cup of coffee. She returns to the office and reads her emails. She sits down and starts to answer them.

Then she switches off the computer and goes to the kitchen where she prepares the dinner, then turns on the television in the living room. Her boyfriend Lewis often calls her on the telephone. They chat for a short while, and then Carmen washes the dishes and decides to go to bed.

PRACTICE C:

1. Where does Kathy Brown live? She lives in the south of England.
2. What is her flat like and where is it? Her flat is small, clean and tidy and is in Reading city centre.
3. Who does she live with? She lives alone but has a cat.
4. How old is she? She is thirty-five years old.
5. Is she married? No, she is not/ isn´t married.
6. What does she do and where does she work? She is a lawyer and works in a big office near her house.
7. What time does she finish work? She finishes work at seven in the evening.
8. How is she when she arrives home? She is very tired.
9. What is there in her flat? There are two bedrooms, a bathroom, a living room and an office.
10. Why does she go up the stairs? She goes up the stairs because she doesn´t like lifts and and she wants to do more exercise.
11. What does she do when she arrives at the third floor? She takes out her key, opens the door and enters.
12. Who comes to say "hello"? Her cat Luna.
13. What does she do in the office? She turns on the computer.
14. What does she make in the kitchen? She makes a cup of coffee.
15. Where does she read her emails? In the office.

16. What does she do after answering them? She goes to the kitchen and prepares the dinner.
17. Who often calls her on the phone? Her boyfriend Lewis.
18. What does Kathy do after washing the dishes? She decides to go to bed.

www.ingramcontent.com/pod-product-compliance
Lightning Source LLC
Chambersburg PA
CBHW081455040426
42446CB00016B/3246